Anonymous

Canada

Containing Statistical and other Information from Government Sources

and useful Counsels to Emigrants

Anonymous

Canada
Containing Statistical and other Information from Government Sources and useful Counsels to Emigrants

ISBN/EAN: 9783337216207

Printed in Europe, USA, Canada, Australia, Japan

Cover: Foto ©Suzi / pixelio.de

More available books at **www.hansebooks.com**

COLONISTS' HANDBOOKS.

No. 1.

CANADA,

CONTAINING

STATISTICAL AND OTHER INFORMATION FROM GOVERNMENT SOURCES,

AND

USEFUL COUNSELS TO EMIGRANTS.

NEW EDITION,
REVISED THROUGHOUT AND BROUGHT UP TO DATE.

PUBLISHED UNDER THE DIRECTION OF THE TRACT COMMITTEE.

LONDON:
SOCIETY FOR PROMOTING CHRISTIAN KNOWLEDGE;
NORTHUMBERLAND AVENUE, CHARING CROSS, W.C.;
43, QUEEN VICTORIA STREET, E.C.;
26, ST. GEORGE'S PLACE, HYDE PARK CORNER, S.W.
BRIGHTON: 135, NORTH STREET.
1883.

TABLE OF CONTENTS.

MAP OF CANADA.

A FEW WORDS TO EMIGRANTS.

CHAPTER I.

1. It may be taken for granted that the reader of this little book has, for some reason or other, made up his mind to emigrate—to leave, either alone or with his wife and children, his own country and his present way of living, and to seek a new country and enter upon a new way of living elsewhere. He will find in this book, in simple form, a large amount of accurate information on Canada, which is one of the countries offering itself to his choice. This information is supplied by the kindness of the Canadian Government, and may be thoroughly relied upon.

We propose to introduce this by a few friendly suggestions to the emigrant on his *Reasons* for *Emigrating;* the *Qualifications* essential to his *Success;* his *Choice* of the *Country* best suited to him.

2. **Reasons for Emigrating.**—Every emigrant, of course, proposes to " better " himself. He wishes to find *better*—that is, more regular and constant—work; or *better* wages, or a *better* position—that is, a position in which he may be his own master, and have his own land or his own business; or a *better* climate—*i.e.*, a climate more suited to his health. He may have found the competition and the struggle too severe in the old country, and have failed to find anything to do, and he looks, perhaps, for an opening where men are scarcer. Last of all, he may be one who, through idleness, or folly, or vice, or crime, has lost his money, his friends, his character, and has ruined all his chances of success and happiness in this land, and who wishes to lead a *better* life, and thinks he will have a better chance of a fresh start in a new country. All these classes

of persons proposing to emigrate may be nearly sure of
finding what they want in one part or another of the
earth's surface. Many people, however, emigrate from
England every year who have no good reason for doing so
with hope of success. Some are actuated by mere restless-
ness and love of change; others have been deceived by
highly-coloured reports, or unwisely suppose that they are
sure to succeed, because some one else, whose circumstances
may be quite different, has succeeded. One of the objects
of this book is to enable its readers to judge beforehand
whether there is any good reason for hoping that they
would succeed if they were to emigrate. We desire to
prevent disappointment as well as to give sound advice.

3. **Qualifications of an Emigrant.**—Probably, those
who thus wish to leave their country are not men of large
capital. Capital, whether large or small, is, of course, a
very valuable qualification for an emigrant. But it may
be said generally that the classes of emigrants, with or
without capital, to whom the Colonies offer the best
promise of success, are *Farmers, Agricultural Labourers,*
and *Mechanics.* A *Farmer* with a small amount of capital
—say £150 to £500—would naturally look to Canada as
his future home. And, though it is not intended to claim
for Canada alone advantages which other countries may
possess equally with it, his ready money, would, probably,
find a quicker and better return in that great country
than in any other of our more distant possessions.
Besides Farmers and Agriculturists, it should be pointed
out that *Domestic Servants* of good character can almost
always find employment in the colonies. The want of
female labour is strongly felt in a new colony, and such
labour is accordingly valuable and well paid. It may be
observed as a fact, whatever may be the worth of it, that
a large portion of girls of good character, emigrants from
England, marry soon after their arrival; though it would,
of course, be rash to go out with such a view. *Strong
arms* and *quick hands* are of themselves good capital in
most new countries, especially if they are accompanied by
a shrewd head, which knows how to use them. But the
most important of all are the moral qualifications. The

emigrant must have a *cheerful industry* ready to turn itself
to anything, not above any kind of honest work; he must
have *patience* to wait for success, and *courage* to persevere
in spite of difficulties and occasional failures; he must
have *temperance* and *sobriety* to keep his body and mind
fit for his work; he must have *frugality*, to lay by for bad
seasons, or sickness, or old age; and he must have *self-
dependence*, as he will have to think and act for himself
far more in a new country than in an old.

4. **Choice of a New Country.**—But though persons
with such qualifications as those spoken of may be encouraged to emigrate, it is rash and foolish to think that
any country out of England will give equal advantages to
all classes of emigrants, or to suppose that it does not
much matter where a person goes, whether to Canada, or
the United States, or Australia, or New Zealand, if only
he emigrates. Many have come back to this country
bitterly disappointed, and have said that emigration is a
mistake; whereas the mistake has been their own, in not
considering carefully where they would find the circumstances best suited to them. Emigration is a step
generally taken once for all. It can only be retraced with
great loss and difficulty, and, therefore, the greatest care
should be used that it be not a false step. An intending
emigrant should not be satisfied with hearing that So-
and-so went out to Australia and made his fortune. He
must consider his own wants, and what his means and
powers are; and then find out where he can employ those
means and powers to the best advantage. Now, there is
a large number of new countries open to a man, each of
them, perhaps, having something to recommend it. How
can he find out which will suit him? If he has sensible
friends who have already gone out, who know what he is
and what he can do, they may be able to advise him. But,
failing this, there are in London representatives of nearly
all the English colonies and dependencies, and the foreign
countries, which have openings for emigrants. Most of
these publish short papers giving the latest information
about the state of the countries which they represent,
showing what inducements are offered to emigrants in the

way of free grants of land or a free or assisted passage, what tradesmen or mechanics are most likely to find employment, what is the current rate of wages, what food is to be had, and what is the price of it and of the other necessaries of life. Besides this present book, others will shortly be issued from the same source with information about other countries. Government or other official advertisements are from time to time inserted in the newspapers asking for mechanics or men skilled in certain trades who are especially wanted in one colony or another, and pointing out the advantages offered in the way of a free or assisted passage, and the wages to be earned. Articles are occasionally printed in the *Times* and other newspapers by persons who have visited or resided in some of the countries open to emigrants, from which much may be learnt about the prospects of trade, or agriculture, or other industries in those countries. If the person intending to emigrate has not the opportunity of seeing these papers, and does not himself know how to get the information which he needs, he should not hesitate to go to the clergyman of his parish, or any clergyman of whom he knows anything, and ask his assistance in learning what he wants. The Rev. J. Bridger, Emigrants' Chaplain, St. Nicholas' Church, Liverpool, will also answer as far as possible inquiries addressed to him by intending emigrants, or by clergy on their behalf.

5. **The Emigrant leaving Home** and on the **Voyage.**—Let it be supposed that the emigrant has chosen his new country, and secured his passage. From the information he has obtained he will, according to his means, have provided himself with the most useful tools, utensils, and other necessaries for his new home. He should certainly not forget to take a *Bible* and *Prayer Book*, and two or three other good books. He will have time to use them on the voyage out. He will find it very useful to provide himself with a letter of commendation from his clergyman to be presented to any clergyman who may be nearest to the spot in which he settles. A form for such a letter will be found at p. 59 of this book. A clergyman would readily copy it out and fill up the

blanks; or he might get a form from the Society which publishes this book, the address of which is to be found on the title-page. With such a letter, which he should take care to use at once, he will always make sure of a friend ready to welcome him on his arrival, and a friend who is likely to be well-informed, and sure to be disinterested and trustworthy. He may also have the advantage of a chaplain on the ship. Let him by all means make a friend of him. He will certainly have many idle hours on his hands during the voyage, and will find himself in the midst of very varied company, some of it not very good. If he has any money, or money's worth, he will very likely be invited to gamble it or drink it away on the ship or as soon as he lands; or he may be persuaded to join in some speculation or scheme or adventure, honest or dishonest, in which he is told that he is sure to make his fortune, but in which he will have to begin by parting with what he has. He must take care not to be caught in any of these traps. He will have many opportunities of showing that he is made of good stuff by obeying all rules and regulations made by the ship's officers. Let him determine to show himself always for the side of order, good humour, unselfishness, friendliness. Above all, if he has the happiness of being a religious man, let him not be ashamed of it, but so show it that he may encourage others.

6. **Arrival.**—On his arrival and during his land journey the emigrant is sure to be beset by a host of so-called agents. It is to be hoped that he will have made up his mind beforehand where to go and what to do, and that he will not allow himself to be turned aside from his plan. He should push forward to his destination, so as to waste no time or money on the way. He will find it quite long and costly enough. If he should be in any doubt, he should look out for a clergyman, who will be sure to advise him well. If he should happen to be going to Manitoba or the North-west he will find a society with many officers, whose express object is to befriend in every possible way new settlers like himself. He will find particulars of this society, which is called the Church of England Settlers'

Society, on pp. 49–52. He will be sure of a friendly hand from members of this society. It may be hoped that similar societies will soon be formed all over the world.

7. **Health.**—The climate and the open air life he will lead will be in favour of the emigrant's health. But he may be far away from any doctor or medicine, and illness to himself or his family would be a far more serious calamity than in the old country. A few hints will be found at p. 55, attention to which may save him from some dangers.

8. **Education.**—The emigrant with a family should not be so cruel to his children as to allow them to grow up without education. Happily in Canada, as is shown at p. 49, there is an opportunity of giving this advantage in life to all of them.

9. **The Emigrant as a Member of Society and of the State.**—There may be some temptation to a man who has come to win a living and a home for himself and his family in a new land to think of that, and that only, and to forget that he is a part of a new society, and a new nation. He should, of course, not waste his time or neglect his business. But it is not good for man to live alone. Men are made for mutual help, and to form societies. They can do things when they are working together that none can do alone. The new-comer ought, therefore, from the first, to try to establish and maintain friendly intercourse with his neighbours; to take and give help; to interest himself in all that concerns and interests them; to use his vote, if he has one, or whatever power he has, for the good of the State to which he belongs, and of his fellow-citizens; to do all he can to support and maintain a good and orderly Government; to show himself a *true patriot*, by helping to get righteous laws and worthy institutions, and to form good customs for those that shall come after him.

10. **The Emigrant as a Churchman.**—In whatever other sense he is a Churchman, there can be scarcely a doubt that the reader has received baptism from the Church, and thus been made a "member of Christ" and of His Church. He has, perhaps, been married in church.

He has grown up within sight or sound of a parish church, and has had the right to the services of *his* clergyman— one who really belonged to him and in whom he had a right—whether he chose to use them or not. He will not find an *established* church in his new country. He will not find the old ivy-grown village church, or the handsome town church, with its bright decorations and beautiful singing, and its doors open to all. But he will find the CHURCH everywhere—that great body, with its bishops and clergy, who have had their commission handed down to them from CHRIST Himself, who minister the sacraments which He ordained and all other means of grace. As a Churchman, the emigrant should not think that the "Church" is only a religion for England, and that he must look out for another religion in Canada or other places. Let him be staunch and faithful to his Church and its Lord. He will find that he has his bishop and his Church clergyman wherever he goes (see "Ecclesiastical Information," p. 48). And if the latter lives a long way off, and there is no church building and no regular service yet established where he is, he should join with those living near him to get one as soon as they can. Till they get their own church and regular service, they should arrange to meet in each others' houses Sunday by Sunday, and read through the service together. He will be a true friend to his neighbours who has the courage to start this habit. Let the Sunday be regularly and religiously observed. It has been found by experience to be almost as great a temporal blessing as it is a spiritual. Our advice would be :—Go regularly to church, and especially to the Holy Communion. Take the earliest opportunity of having your children baptised. Let your children go to Sunday School, if there be one within reach; if not, teach them the Catechism and give them a Bible lesson at home. Have your children confirmed as soon as they are old enough. Gather your family together for family prayer every morning and evening. Never omit your own daily private prayer (for some prayers for your own use see pp. 59–64) and the daily reading of the Bible, if it be but a few verses. Bring up your children in the habit of prayer.

and **Bible** reading. Support and help your **bishop and clergy in all** their efforts for your own **and your neighbours' good.** Religion will bring brightness **and comfort** to your own heart and home, and a strong **church will be** a strong backbone to the nation.

CHAPTER II.

SOME ACCOUNT OF THE DOMINION OF CANADA.

1. Description.—The Dominion of Canada **is bounded** on the south by the United States of America, and extends from the Atlantic to the Pacific Ocean. Its area is 3,470,392 square miles, and its most southern point reaches the 42nd parallel of latitude. · It possesses **thousands of** square miles of the finest forests on the continent, **widely** spread coal fields, extensive and productive **fisheries, and** rivers and lakes that are among the largest and most remarkable in the world. The country is divided into eight provinces, the names of which are given below:—

1. Nova Scotia ... ... containing 20,907 sq. miles.
2. New Brunswick ... ,, 27,174 ,,
3. Prince Edward Island ,, 2,133 ,,
4. Quebec ... ... ,, 188,688 ,,
5. Ontario ... ... ,, 101,733 ,,
6. Manitoba ... ... ,, 123,200 ,,
7. North-West Territories ,, 2,665,252 ,,
8. British Columbia ... ,, 341,305 ,,

2. Population.—According to the census taken in 1881 the population of the Dominion at that time numbered 4,324,810. Of these Nova Scotia contained 440,572; New Brunswick, 321,233; Prince Edward Island, 108,891; Quebec, 1,359,027; Ontario, 1,923,228; Manitoba, 65,954; North-West Territories, 56,446; British Columbia, 49,459. The origins of the populations are returned as follows:— 891,248 English and Welsh, 957,408 Irish, 699,863 Scotch,

1,298,929 French, 254,319 German. The balance is made up of Dutch, Scandinavians, Italians, etc. The tables of the birthplaces of the inhabitants show that there are at the present time living in Canada 77,753 persons who were born in the United States.

3. **Government.**—The government of the country is administered by a representative of her Majesty, whose official title is Governor-General. The tenure of the office is six years, and the expenses are borne by the Dominion. The Federal Parliament includes a Senate and a House of Commons, and legislates upon all questions affecting the general welfare of the country. The members of the Senate are elected for life, but they can resign at any time. The House of Commons is composed of representatives from every part of Canada. The government is conducted on the English basis of the responsibility of the Ministers to Parliament, which is elected for a term of five years. The government of the Provinces is carried on by Lieutentant-Governors, appointed by the Governor-General in Council, and local legislatures, which deal with civil rights and property, the administration of justice, and local matters, such as education, control of lands and municipal institutions, prisons, asylums, etc. The Provinces are further subdivided into counties and townships, with local boards and councils for regulating taxation for roads, schools, and municipal purposes. The franchise is practically extended to every householder.

4. **Education.**—The educational system is under the control of the various provinces. Free schools are provided, and facilities are afforded to successful pupils for obtaining the highest education. (See also p. 49.)

5. **Militia.**—The defence of the country is entrusted to the militia, which consists of two forces, the active and the reserve. The strength of the former is fixed by law at 40,000, service in which is voluntary. In the latter all male British subjects between the ages of 16 and 60, not exempted or disqualified by law, are liable to be called upon to serve in case of emergency. The active militia, armed with breech-loading rifles, is equipped in much the

same manner as the volunteers and the militia of England, and can be placed in the field at a short notice. It is called out for a number of days' drill every year, for which the officers and men are paid. Commissions are given to persons who have graduated in the military colleges, and to persons who have the necessary experience, and are able to pass the qualifying examinations. The force is under the command of a general officer of the English army. In many of the universities, colleges, normal and high schools, associations are organized for the purposes of military drill. They are supplied by the Government with arms and accoutrements. Instruction is given in military drill and training only, and the companies so formed are not to be employed in active service. No person can be appointed an officer in the active militia, except provisionally, until he has obtained a certificate of fitness from one of the military schools of the Dominion or a board of officers of the active militia to be constituted as her Majesty may appoint. There is a military college for the education of cadets (with a four years' course of study) at Kingston, and schools of gunnery at Quebec and Kingston.

6. **Trade.**—Every facility is offered for securing patents for inventions, the fees being very moderate, while the protection is as effective as in other countries.

The following figures show the imports and exports of Canada for the fiscal year ended June 30, 1881 :—

Imports	$91,611,604
Exports	98,290,823

The exports are divided thus :—

Produce of the mines	$2,916,254
„ „ fisheries	6,898,884
„ „ forests	25,709,848
Animals and their products ...	22,665,610
Agricultural produce	31,294,127
Manufactures	4,043,123
Miscellaneous articles, coin and bullion, and estimated amount short returned at inland ports	4,962,977

Agriculture forms the principal wealth of the Dominion at the present time ; but it will be seen that Canada is taking a place as a manufacturing country, and its re- sources are such as to justify the statement that its growth in this respect is likely to continue. Since 1878 the value of the imports from Great Britain has increased from $37,431,000 to $43,583,000 in 1881, and they are equal now to about £2 sterling per capita, as compared with 14s. 9d. per capita in the United States. The pro- portion in favour of Canada would be still greater if manufactures only were taken into consideration, showing the relative importance of the development of Canada to Great Britain, both as providing homes for her surplus population and an extended market for her manufactures.

7. **Climate.**—In a country like the Dominion of Canada, extending northward from the 42nd parallel of latitude, and east to west for 3000 miles, the climate is naturally variable ; but, to speak generally, the summers are hotter than in England, and the winters colder. But neither the summer heat nor the winter cold are disad- vantageous to the inhabitants or to the productiveness of the land. The warmth of the summer months extends the range of production in grains from oats and barley to wheat and maize ; in fruits, from apples and pears to peaches, grapes, melons, nectarines, and apricots ; and in vegetables, from potatoes, turnips, carrots, and cabbages, to the egg plant and tomatoes. The winter temperature cannot properly be measured by the thermometer for purposes of comparison with that of other countries. It is at times much below zero ; but the air is so dry, and so exhilarating, that its effect upon the body is not nearly so great as a much higher temperature would be in a more humid climate. To agriculture, snow and ice are no great drawbacks. They mean protection to the land almost as valuable as a covering of manure. They con- vert the surface of the earth into roads equal to turnpikes in any direction, over which millions of tons of produce of all kinds are transported at a minimum cost, affording employment for men and horses when cultivation is arrested by the frost. Besides, from an agricultural point

of view, whether the thermometer is at freezing point or
whether it is below zero is a matter of small moment.
The winter in Canada has little or no effect upon vegetation. The fruit trees remain practically uncared for
during the season; ferns, flowers, and shrubs appear
every spring as regularly as they do in England, and the
woods and valleys abound in wild fruits. Grape vines in
the Ottawa valley and in the Toronto and other districts
are left unprotected during the winter without injury.
It is also stated that Canada cannot be a cattle-raising
country. Yet not only does it produce sufficient for its
four and a half millions of inhabitants, but large numbers
are exported every year. It should be borne in mind in
this connection that cattle are not permitted to enter
Canada from the United States, except pedigree stock for
breeding purposes, and this concession has only been
granted a few months. This does not apply to Manitoba
and the North-West Territories, from which, however, no
cattle are at present exported; but there are in those
districts ranches containing many thousand head of stock
which are not sheltered during the winter. The following figures show the export of Canadian cattle, horses,
and sheep, during the last three years :—

	Cattle.	Horses.	Sheep.
1879	46,569	16,629	308,093
1880	54,944	21,393	398,746
1881	62,277	·21,993	354,155

Blodgett, the American climatologist, speaking of the
climate of Canada says:—

" But the lower annual mean detracts little or nothing
from the productive capacity of Canada, the greater heat
of summer fully compensating for the cold of winter ; and
there are large districts in the East, with still greater
areas on the Pacific Coast, which possess all the advantages of full maritime climates. Nova Scotia, with a
portion of New Brunswick and several ·adjacent islands,
possess what may be called a full maritime climate, or
one with a very moderate curve of changes in successive
months, and no conspicuous extremes of heat and cold. . . .

Another most important and distinctive climatological district is found on the plains east of the Rocky Mountains, in which the maritime features blend with a continental, affording a climate analagous to that of the plains of South Russia, and highly favourable to agriculture and fixed occupation of the soil. The modified climate extends westward from Lake Superior and Lake Winnipeg to the Rocky Mountains, and indeed beyond them in various cultivatable valleys; the general area being a triangle, with its base along the 49th parallel, its western arm along the 122nd meridian of longitude from 49° to 60° north latitude, from which point a nearly right line to Fort William would form its north-easterly arm . . . over which the general climate is as favourable as that of Prussia, or as that of South Russia from Moscow to the Black Sea."

It.is not necessary to point out that the winter cold in Canada is greater than in England. That is an admitted fact; but it is not disadvantageous. The houses in Canada, and the clothes worn, are adapted to the weather, and it is well known that Canadians prefer their dry, clear, winter weather, to the damp, cutting temperature that prevails in England. It is said that farmers cannot work in winter, and that labour is at a standstill. A greater mistake could not be made. A farmer, in Canada, does very much the same work in the winter as an English farmer in the same season and in wet weather. While the frost stays actual cultivation, which at the outside is only about five months, and often less—in 1881, ploughing was being done in the Ottawa district on the last day of December—employment is found for men and horses in carting, and in many other ways. Lumbering is also done during the winter, and absorbs a large number of men. Mechanics can continue work during the season, excepting such men as masons and bricklayers, and even they can do inside work. But if a man goes to a colony, he must be prepared to take what work is available, and, in Canada, no difficulty in securing employment will be found by any man who is willing to work.

8. **Means of Communication.**—Canada has an ex-

tensive railway system. There are about 8000 miles in
operation, affording means of communication from the
province of Nova Scotia to the western portions of Ontario, and again from the western shores of Lake Superior
into Manitoba and the North-West Territory. The
Canadian Pacific Railway—one of the greatest national
undertakings of the age—is being rapidly constructed.
It is already in operation from Thunder Bay on Lake
Superior to Winnipeg and 500 miles west of that city,
and from Winnipeg south to the international boundary,
where it connects with the United States railways. It is
confidently expected that in 1886 there will be a railway
from the Maritime Provinces to the Pacific Coast entirely
through Canadian territory, the importance of which to
the country and to the British Empire it is impossible
to exaggerate. The Canadian Pacific Railway deserves
special mention. Prior to 1880 the work of making a
connection between the Atlantic and Pacific coasts was
being carried out by the Government; but in that year
it was transferred to a syndicate, which is now engaged
in rapidly constructing the line. There are 1000 miles
of it in operation at the present time, and the track has
been laid during the past season at the rate of between
two and three miles per day. It is now open to within
300 miles of the Rocky Mountains, and the difficult work
in British Columbia and on the northern shore of Lake
Superior is also being accelerated as much as possible.
The line, when complete, will be 2600 miles long. This
does not include the branches that will be inevitable.
The public importance of the railway will be understood
when it is stated that a subsidy in already completed
works and in cash, equal to nearly eleven millions sterling,
and twenty-five millions of acres of land, was voted by
the Canadian Parliament to enable the contract to be
carried out. The land will of course be sold by the Company for colonization purposes.

The inland navigation of the Dominion has cost a large
sum of money, but it is a work of which the country may
well be proud. Vessels of 600 tons can proceed from the
western end of Lake Superior, and from the United States

ports of that vast inland sea, to Montreal by way of Lakes
Michigan, Huron, Erie, and Ontario, and the river St.
Lawrence—a distance of nearly 1300 miles. The locks
on the Welland Canal connecting Lakes Erie and Ontario
—rendered necessary by the Niagara Falls—have recently
been enlarged, and are now 270 feet long, 45 feet wide,
and 14 feet deep. Vessels of a still larger size will therefore be used to carry produce direct from Western Canada
and the United States to the St. Lawrence route, which
will tend to cheapen the cost of transport. The Canadian
route from the lakes to the ports of transhipment compared with that to New York and other American ports
possesses some advantages. Take, for instance, the distance from Chicago. It is 150 miles less to Montreal
than it is to New York, *via* Buffalo and Erie Canal, and
there are sixteen more locks and 89½ feet more lockage by
the American than by the Canadian route. In addition,
Montreal is 300 miles nearer to England than New York.
To show the improvement that has taken place in the
navigation of the St. Lawrence, it may be stated that in
1850 the channel between Quebec and Montreal was only
11 feet deep; it has gradually been increased to 26 feet.
Atlantic steamers of 5000 tons can now be moored alongside the wharves at the latter city.

9. **Postal and Telegraph Arrangements.**—Canada
possesses excellent postal arrangements, a post-office being
found in almost every village; and every place of any importance is connected with the electric telegraph.

10. **Emigration to Canada.**—(*a*) **Classes of Emigrants.**—Emigration into Canada for some years past has
been of a very satisfactory character. The figures given
below will show the number of persons who have left Great
Britain for Canada since 1879. They do not include those
who travelled direct from the Continent of Europe to Canada;
those who travelled *via* New York; or those who left the
United States to take up their homes in the Dominion.

1880	...	...	...	...	...	29,202
1881	...	...	...	...	...	34,239
1882 (up to September 30th)				...	46,739

The increase in the numbers from year to year is in itself evidence of the great prosperity which the Colony is enjoying. For some time past it has been a fallacy that a very large emigration takes place from Canada to the United States. This has arisen from the publication of statistics from American sources. The statements have been analysed in a report made to the Canadian Government by the Secretary of the Department of Agriculture, and recently presented to both Houses of Parliament in England. It shows conclusively that the figures are based upon incorrect information, and cannot be supported. There is naturally a considerable movement of people between Canada and the United States, as the countries adjoin one another, but any emigration from the one is counterbalanced by the emigration from the other. The contrary impressions promulgated have tended to prejudice Canada in the eyes of intending emigrants, but without much effect, as the foregoing figures demonstrate.

The classes recommended to emigrate are as follows :—

1. Tenant-farmers in the United Kingdom with sufficient capital to enable them to settle on farms may be advised to go with safety, and with the certainty of doing well. The same remark applies to persons able to adapt themselves to agricultural pursuits, and having sufficient means to purchase farms.

2. Persons with capital seeking investment.

3. Male and female farm labourers, female domestic servants, mechanics, and labourers, to whom assisted passages are granted.

The classes warned against emigration are females above the grade of servants, clerks, shopmen, and persons having no particular trade or calling, and unaccustomed to manual labour. To these Canada offers but little encouragement.

Questions are frequently asked as to the prospects of civil engineers, surveyors, doctors, and clerks in Canada, and as to commissions in the Canadian Militia, the batteries of Artillery, and the North-West Mounted Police. Generally speaking, professional gentlemen, and those following the lighter callings, are not advised to proceed to Canada on the chance of securing employment of the kind they have been accustomed to. It is found that the supply of such persons is equal to the demand, and some hesitation is felt in recommending them to go out, unless to fill appointments they have previously secured. This is a general statement, and instances could of course be produced where such men have gone to the country and succeeded. But very much depends upon the persons themselves. A doctor will find no difficulty in practising in Canada if he has an English diploma, and the same remark applies to a surveyor, civil engineer, or a barrister; but they should have some money to rely upon for a time. English solicitors have to serve for a year in an attorney's office before being allowed to practise. With regard to commissions in the Militia and Artillery of Canada, such appointments are generally given to persons who have passed through the Canadian Military Colleges, or to those possessing local influence and the necessary knowledge, a qualifying examination having to be passed. The North-West Mounted Police is recruited solely in Canada. It numbers from 400 to 500 men, and its duty consists in keeping order in the North-West Territories of Canada. Recruits must be unmarried, not less than 18 years of age, and not more than 40. The minimum chest measurement is 35 inches, and the maximum weight 175 pounds. The pay ranges from 40 cents per day to 70 cents, according to service. The engagement is for five years. The force is clothed, mounted, and maintained by the Government. Commissions are, as far as possible, given according to merit; but such appointments are also given to cadets of the Military Colleges, and to other persons whose experience especially qualifies them for the duties.

The classes of men particularly wanted in the Dominion are agriculturists, farmers, farm labourers, general labourers, navvies, mechanics, and last, but not least, domestic servants. Persons with capital will find opportunities for the safe investment of money, not excelled in any other part of the world. Manufacturers receive every

encouragement from municipalities in the establishment
of factories, and in many cases are exempted from taxation
for a time; while the general information conveyed in
this pamphlet shows the prospects that are open to the
other classes. With regard to domestic servants, the
following extracts from letters from the Government
agents in the different parts of Canada will be interesting :—

Toronto.—" The average wages paid to general servants
are $7 per month, the higher being about $8 and the
lower $5. The demand for servant girls is very large."
St. John, *N.B.* — " Girls capable of becoming general
domestic servants, and able to do plain cooking, washing,
sweeping, etc., in small families where only one servant is
kept, can obtain wages ranging from $6 to $8 per month.
The demand for this class of servant is large. Cooks
command from $8 to $12."—*Montreal.*—" I am enabled
to report that wages range as follows, good servants being
in great demand :—Good cooks, $14 to $16 per month;
plain cooks, $10 to $12; parlour-maids, $8 to $10;
house and parlour-maids, $7 to $9; head nurses, $9 to
$12; second nurses, $5 to $7; good general servants,
$8 to $10; kitchen maids, $6 to $8; laundresses, $9 to
$12; maids and general country servants, $6 to $10.
We could place a great many in this district." *Hamilton.*
—" During the last season we have been unable to supply
the demand, hundreds of applicants being disappointed.
One train arriving here brought thirty girls. We found
situations for the whole of them within one hour, and
could have disposed of double the number. Wages—
Inexperienced girls, for country, $3 to $5 per month;
fair general servants, for city, $5 to $7; good general
servants, $8 to $9; cooks, $8 to $10; housemaids, $7
to $8." *Winnipeg, Manitoba.*—" Servants who understand
or who are willing to learn work in a Canadian house are
in great demand, and find employment as soon as they
arrive, at wages from $10 to $15 per month in private
houses. In boarding houses and hotels some servants
secure from $12 to $30 per month; experienced cooks
get from $15 to $25, while in hotels, $25 to $35 is paid,

but the demand is limited. Dressmakers are paid from
$25 to $40 per month, but have to provide for themselves." *London, Ontario.*—"A large number of female
domestic servants could secure situations in this district.
It would be desirable to bring testimonials. Wages—Cooks,
$8 to $10 per month; housemaids, $5 to $7; general
servants, $6 to $8; laundresses, $10 to $12; nurse girls,
$3 to $5; sewing girls get from 50 to 60 cents per day."
Ottawa.—"The demand for female domestics amounted
this season to 750 applications, the supply was only 126.
Wages range from $4 to $10 per month, according to
value of service rendered. Intelligent girls, accustomed
to household duties, such as washing, ironing, and plain
cooking, readily command $6 to $8 per month, and good
fair cooks from $8 to $10." *Kingston.*—"It is impossible
to state the number of well-trained and competent female
servants that could find employment, being urgently
needed in every city, farm, and village, and in the rural
districts among the farming community, and might be
numbered by thousands. Wages, according to capacity,
from $4 to $8 per month. Average wages, say from
$5.50 to $6 per month."

It must be stated in regard to these figures, as well as
those relating to rates of wages and cost of living under
the heading of the different provinces, that they are
subject to alteration from time to time, as in every other
country. They are only published so as to give a general
idea upon the matter to persons who frequently ask for
such information.

(*b*) **Time to Emigrate.**—The best time to leave Great
Britain for Canada is about the middle of April. This
applies more particularly to persons who have no friends
in the country. Those who have, may be safely advised
to go out earlier. They will no doubt be informed upon
this point, and receive direct information for their guid-
ance. Persons are not encouraged to emigrate to Canada
in the winter, for the reason that business of all kinds
is slacker during that season than others, just the same as
in any other country. In the spring everything is active,
and permanent employment obtainable.

CHAPTER III.

THE PROVINCES OF CANADA.

IT is now proposed to offer a few remarks on each of the different provinces of which the Dominion of Canada is composed.

(A) MANITOBA AND THE NORTH-WEST TERRITORIES.

1. General Description.—The country now universally known under the above names, was granted by Charter to the Hudson Bay Company in 1670, during the reign of Charles II., as a hunting and trading ground, and was held by it, and by the North-West Company (the two corporations amalgamated in 1821) until 1870, when their rights were surrendered to the Dominion. It has been a matter for surprise that so fertile a region should, for a long period, have been comparatively lost to the world, but the facts that are mentioned will, no doubt, enable an intelligible conclusion to be arrived at. However, since the transfer took place, the country has been advancing by leaps and bounds, and, in 1882, must contain nearly 200,000 people. In 1870 it had no railway communication, practically no towns or villages, few post-offices, and no connection with the telegraph. Now everything is changed. Its principal city, Winnipeg, contains probably 25,000 people, and there are many other places rapidly rising into prominence, with populations ranging from a few hundreds to thousands. The province has two railway lines running south, connecting with the United States systems, and one line to Thunder Bay, on Lake Superior, and the Canadian Pacific Railway is constructed 500 miles west of Winnipeg. Besides, the Red River is navigable for a considerable distance; there are 1200 miles of navigation on the Saskatchewan, and vessels trade on the Assiniboine River as far as Fort Ellice. There are nearly 200 post-offices in the country, and telegraphic communication. Manitoba is the name of a province formed out of the North-West Territories. It is situated between the parallels 49°–50° 50′ latitude N., and 89°–102° west longitude, in the centre of the American continent. It contains about 123,200 square miles, or 78,000,000 acres of land. An Order in Council was passed during the year 1882, dividing the North-West Territories beyond the confines of Manitoba into four new districts, or, more properly speaking, territories, as follows :—

Assiniboia, containing about 95,000 square miles, is bounded on the south by the international boundary, on the east by the western boundary of Manitoba, on the north by a line drawn near 52° latitude, and on the west by a line drawn between 110° and 111° west longitude ; Saskatchewan, containing 114,000 square miles, is bounded on the south by Assiniboia, on the east by Lake Winnipeg and Nelson River, on the north by a line drawn near 55° latitude, and on the west by a continuation of the line marking that boundary of the previous district ; Alberta, containing 100,000 square miles, is bounded on the south by the international boundary, on the east by Assiniboia and Saskatchewan, on the west by British Columbia, and on the north by the continuation of the line bounding Saskatchewan ; Athabasca, containing about 122,000 square miles, is bounded on the south by Alberta, on the west by British Columbia, on the east by the line bounding Assiniboia to the west until it intersects Athabasca River, then by it and the lake of the same name, and following Slave Lake to a line near 60° latitude, which forms the northern boundary. To sum up, Saskatchewan district includes the towns of Battleford, Carleton, and Prince Albert. Assiniboia includes Qu'appelle, South Saskatchewan and Souris Rivers, and Forts Pelly and Ellice. The principal town is Regina, on the Wascana River, and is estimated to contain nearly 1000 people. The site was only selected this year. Alberta includes the Battle, Bow, and Belly Rivers, the cattle ranche district, the towns of Edmonton, Calgary, and Fort McLeod ; and Athabasca takes in the celebrated Peace River district. The division of the vast country, hitherto known as the Great North West, will have the effect of localizing points which hitherto were very indefinitely comprehended, and, by having each its capital assigned it, will form nuclei for settlements.

2. Free Grants of Land.—Any male or female who is the head of a family, or any person who has attained the age of 18 years, can obtain a free grant of a quarter section of 160 acres; and can also make an entry for pre-emption rights to the adjoining quarter section, at the Government price ranging from S2 per acre upwards.

3. The New Dominion Lands Act.—The following is a summary of the latest regulations for the disposal of public lands in Manitoba and the North-West Territories:—

The country is surveyed into " townships " of six miles square, each containing 36 square mile lots or sections. These sections are numbered consecutively 1 to 36; two in each township are reserved to defray the expenses of education, and are sold by auction from time to time, and two others belong to the Hudson Bay Company, which Corporation offers its lands for sale at prices ranging from 14s. to 24s. per acre, on deferred payments. The London office of the Hudson's Bay Company is at 1, Lime Street, E.C. For 24 miles on each side of the railway (now being made) across the continent, the remainder of the odd-numbered sections in each township belong to the Canadian·Pacific Railway Company, who dispose of their large land grants on favourable terms of purchase. Full particulars can be obtained at the London office of the Company, 101, Cannon Street, E.C. The remaining even-numbered sections in each township (16) are held exclusively by the Government for free grant and pre-emption purposes. These sections are each subdivided into four quarter sections of 160 acres, two being available for free grants, and two for pre-emptions. Any male or female who is at the head of a family, any male member of a family 18 years old, or any other person who has attained that age, can obtain a free grant of 160 acres, and can also make an entry for pre-emption rights to the adjoining 160 acres at the Government price of S2.50 per acre, payable in cash at the end of three years.

For office fees to cover the cost of survey, documents, etc., a charge of $10 is made in each case at the time of entry. Outside the railway belt alluded to above, the even-numbered sections are also held for free grants and pre-emptions, the odd-numbered being designated "public lands." Such pre-emptions and public lands are offered for sale by the Government at $2 per acre, the money in the former case being paid at the end of three years, and in the latter at the time of purchase. The title to the free grant is given at the end of three years. The conditions to be fulfilled are: residence on the land six months annually for three years; the erection of a house; and the general cultivation of the land, but the settler is not bound to put any specified quantity under crops.

Settlers having no wood on their lands are permitted to purchase timber lots in area not exceeding 20 acres, at $5 per acre, to be paid in cash.

Special and advantageous arrangements are made for the sale of tracts of land to Companies or to individuals having in view the colonization of the country, upon certain conditions, with powers of protection for advances made to settlers on free grant lands to the extent of £100.

Tracts of lands, in no case to exceed 100,000 acres, are also leased for pasturage purposes at a rent of £2 per annum for each thousand acres, upon certain conditions. The lessee also acquires the power to purchase five per cent. of the area of the leasehold for buildings, etc., at $1.25 per acre, payable upon purchase.

4. Guides.—Intending settlers should go at once to the land office in the district where they intend to settle, and guides will be sent with them, free of charge, to point out vacant lands available for settlement.

5. Capital Required.—Questions are often asked as to the amount of capital considered necessary to enable a man and his family to start farming on a free grant of land. The result of experience tends to show that a man may make a fair beginning if possessed of from £100 to £120, and his position ought to get better every year, with a gradually extending area under cultivation. A man's success is measured more or less by his own exertions. It is difficult to lay down a hard and fast rule as to the amount of money required. The above estimate is based upon the assumption that all payments for goods are to be made on delivery, but a settler could obtain many of his requirements on credit until such time as his first crops were harvested. It is fair to assume that a much lower sum would really suffice, as a settler and his family with little capital would command a good price for their labour during harvest time and in any spare moments. This would add to the means of such a family, and help to keep them going until they had a sufficient quantity of their own land under cultivation to keep them fully occupied. It is scarcely necessary to say that the more money a settler has the better his chances are of getting on rapidly; but many men landing in Canada with only a pound or two in their pockets have taken up the free grants, have hired themselves out to labour, cultivating their own land during spare time, and employing a man at harvest or when necessary. In this way they have stocked and cultivated their farms. There are many men in Canada now in positions of independence who commenced in this way. It will be understood that the figures named above do not include the passage of the settler and his family from England to Manitoba and the North-West.

Farming implements and tools can be obtained in all parts of Canada as cheaply as in England, so that it is not worth the while of a settler to take such things with him. The same remark applies to furniture and household utensils. A good supply of clothes may safely be taken, as well as blankets, unfilled bedding, linen, and articles of that nature, but the fact must be borne in mind that the railway companies fix as limits for the free conveyance of baggage, 250 lbs. for each first-class, and 100 lbs. for third-class passengers.

Special railway fares are in existence for persons who desire to take through tickets to Winnipeg. The cost of reaching Canada is explained on p. 52. The all-rail route is by way of Toronto, Chicago, and St. Paul to Winnipeg. The lake route is by way of Sarnia or Collingwood, whence the boats depart for Thunder Bay (and Duluth), at the Western end of Lake Superior. The Canadian Pacific Railway is open thence to Winnipeg. The journey takes about five days, and the passenger has to provide his own provisions on the way. The trains stop at several places on the way for refreshments, where meals can be obtained at various prices from 1*s.* upwards, or a settler can take his own provisions. The advice of the Government Agent at the port of landing can be obtained on this point. About 1000 miles of the Canadian Pacific Railway is now in operation from Thunder Bay (Lake Superior) to Winnipeg, thence to the boundary line, and from Winnipeg westward for 500 miles. The railway will pass through extensive coal-fields, and will also open up extensive forests in the Lake Superior District and near the Rocky Mountains, the timber of which will be very valuable to settlers in the country. By either of these routes settlers may be met by interested persons who may endeavour to persuade settlement in the United States as preferable to Canada. No notice should be taken of them, and settlers are advised to proceed without deviation to their destination.

6. **Cost of Breaking up Land.**—The cost of breaking up the prairie land is estimated at three dollars per acre, and the ploughing, sowing, harvesting, and threshing, the second year, four dollars per acre.

7. **Improved Farms.**—Improved farms can be purchased from £1 per acre upwards.

8. **Cost of Living, Demand for Labour, and Wages Paid.**—The following information, taken from recent Winnipeg papers, will be interesting, as giving a general idea of the trade of the city, rates of wages, and cost of living. They are subject to alteration from time to time as in any other country, and must be valued accordingly. With regard to the second point, the figures naturally become higher as the season nears its close, owing to the anxiety to get works in hand finished; but this should not cause persons to emigrate late in the autumn for some years to come.

"Notwithstanding that this is one of the dullest periods of the season (October) trade in all its branches continues very brisk. The imports are larger than ever before; large orders continue to be received from the country; the splendid harvest has created an enthusiastic feeling among all classes of the people, and a trade of unprecedented and undreamed-of proportions is now looked forward to. Scores of new stores are being opened, or will be opened within the next six weeks, on Main and other leading streets. Some of these will be among the finest in the city. Trade with the United States and England continues to increase, as is shown in the following comparative statement for the eight months ending August 31st:—

Eight months' trade, 1881 ...	...	$1,820,941
Eight months' trade, 1882 ...	...	5,260,378
Increase 1882 over 1881 ...	...	3,439,437

"The largest items of imports were lumber and manufactures of wood, cotton, live stock, provisions, machinery, fruits, coal, and liquors.

"The market is well supplied with live stock raised in the vicinity of Winnipeg; the supply exceeds the demand. There has been a slight decrease in the price of lambs. The imports from the United States have very materially decreased, the value of animals imported for July and August being $37,800, against $146,315 for the months of May and June. In the course of another year, when the stock farms near Winnipeg commence to send to market the cattle they have raised, it is believed that American importations will entirely cease. The current quotations are:—

Beef, prime ...	... $5.50 to 6.00	per 100 lbs.
Beef, common	... 4.50 to 5.00	,,
Mutton ...	... 6.00 to 7.00	,,
Lambs ...	... 4.00 to 5.00	,,
Hogs	... 8.00 to 9.00	,,

"The retail market is well supplied with all kinds of meats of very good quality. Housekeepers would do well to purchase their winter supplies now. Quarters or sides of beef and hogs can be obtained much cheaper than the current retail prices quoted below.

	Cents.	Cents.
Beef, roast, per lb.		20 to 25
Beef steak, per lb.		20 to 25
Beef, corned, per lb.		12½ to 15
Beef for boiling, per lb.		10 to 12½
Shank, per lb.		5
Liver, per lb.		5
Kidney, per lb.		20
Suet, per lb.		15
Mutton, roast, per lb.		15 to 25
Mutton chop		25
Veal		20 to 25
Pork, per lb.		12½ to 20
Sausages, per lb.		18 to 20
Lard, per lb.		20
Ham, per lb.		20 to 25
Bacon, per lb.		20

'Wild ducks are plentiful, and sell as low as 25c. per pair. Chickens are down to 75c. and $1. Prairie chickens are scarce. A solitary representative of the goose and turkey tribes appeared in the market yesterday, which enables a quotation to be made."

Geese, each	$1.50 to 2.00
Turkeys, per lb.	25 to 30
Chickens, per pair...	75 to 1.00
Prairie chicken	75 to 1.00
Ducks, per pair	75
Wild ducks, per pair	25 to 50

FRESH, PICKLED, AND CANNED FISH.

"Whitefish are scarce. Fresh-water herring are plentiful. There is a good supply of oysters in cans, and the price has dropped to 75c. The first supply of oysters in bulk is expected next week. The demand for codfish, herring, and mackerel is increasing, and will continue to

increase while meat keeps so high. Boneless cod at 12½c.
per lb. goes a long way farther than beef at twice that
price. The maritime provinces send large quantities of
fish to Chicago, which find a ready sale. Consignments
to Winnipeg ought therefore to find a ready market."

		Cents.
Codfish, salt, per lb.		12½
Codfish, boneless, per lb.		12½
Mackerel, pickled, per lb.		10 to 15
Halibut, per lb.		35
Lake Superior Trout, per lb.		15
Salmon, canned		25
Whitefish, smoked, per lb.		15
Whitefish, fresh, per lb.		12½
Herring, fresh-water, per doz. ...		50
Oysters, per can (Gold Seal)		75 to 85
Oysters, canned		25
Lobsters, canned, per lb.		25

LABOUR AND WAGES.

As the winter approaches and the building season
begins to draw to an end labour becomes more plentiful.
A great many men are seeking steady indoor work for the
winter, at wages ranging from $30 to $50 per month.
There is a steady demand for lumbermen at from $30 to
$40 per month. The wages of bricklayers have gone up
to $6 per day. There is a demand for stonemasons from
the west. Female servants are in great demand. Some
hotels are offering as high as $25 per month for good
girls. It is believed that 500 girls could readily find
employment in the city at the present moment.

As pointed out in a previous paragraph, the wages for
mechanics, especially those of the building trades, become
high at the close of the season. Much lower wages pre-
vail in the spring, although even then the money paid is
much higher than in Great Britain.

Winnipeg, although a very young city, is making rapid
strides. Its main street is now lighted by electricity and
traversed by a tramway. There are gasworks, the gas

being made from oil, and waterworks, the service being laid on to such of the houses as are prepared to pay for the convenience. There are doubtless many things to be done yet to add to the comfort of its inhabitants, but they will all come in good time. House rent has been very high during the present season, but when it is stated that the population has doubled in the year it will readily be seen that the resources of the city could not be expected to absorb the largely increased number. However, tent hotels were erected, the public buildings utilized, the emigration sheds extended, and very little trouble has consequently arisen. Persons can remain in the emigration sheds for a time, or rent a plot of land near the city, and put up a shanty if any difficulty is found in securing proper accommodation. It is hoped that before this book is issued some further information on this point—a most important one—will be received.

AVERAGE RATE OF WAGES, COST OF BOARD, AND HOUSE RENT IN THE PROVINCE OF MANITOBA.

Winnipeg and District.—Farm labourers, with board, per month, £4 4s. to £8 8s.; female farm servants, £2 2s. to £3 3s.; general labourers, per day, 8s. to 11s.; railway labourers, 10s. to 12s.; masons, per day, 12s. 6d. to 20s.; bricklayers, 16s. to 25s.; carpenters, 6s. to 16s. 6d.; lumbermen (for shanty), £5 to £7 7s. per month, with board; smiths, per day, 12s. 6d. to 14s. 6d.; wheelwrights, 10s. to 16s.; gardeners, with board, per month, £4 to £6; mill hands, per day, 8s. to 10s.; engine drivers, 12s. to 20s.; saddlers, 8s. to 12s.; bootmakers, 8s. to 12s.; tailors, 12s. to 20s.; female cooks, per month, £3 to £6; domestic servants, £2.10s. to £4;-laundresses, £3 to £5; cost of board, £1 to £1 12s. per week; house rent, for houses of 3 to 5 rooms, £4 to £6 per month; houses of 5 to 7 rooms, £6 to 15 per month.

Brandon District.—Farm labourers, per day, without board, 8s.; per week and board, £1 13s.; general labourers, per day, 8s. to 10s.; railway labourers, 8s.; masons, 12s. to 20s.; bricklayers, 12s. to 20s.; carpenters, 10s. to 16s.;

lumbermen, 8s.; smiths, 8s. to 16s.; gardeners, with
board, 6s.; without board, 8s.; mill hands, 10s. to 14s.;
engine drivers, 14s. to 20s.; saddlers, 10s. to 14s.; bootmakers, 10s. to 14s.; tailors, 8s. to 14s.; female cooks, per
month, £4 to £6; domestic servants, £2 2s. to £3; laundresses, £5 to £6; cost of board, per week, £1; rent, for
small house, £1 12s. per month, and upwards.

9. **Fuel.**—There is not so much woodland in the
prairie district as in other parts of Canada, but there is
enough for the purposes of fuel and fencing, and timber for
building purposes can be purchased in the larger towns
and settlements. Coal also exists in various parts of the
country, and is being worked.

10. **Routes and Internal Communication.**—It may
be mentioned that there are two routes by which an
intending settler can reach Manitoba from Quebec, or any
other Canadian port, namely, the "all rail route," *viâ*
Detroit, Chicago, and St. Paul to Winnipeg, or by what is
called the Lake route, *i.e.* by railway to Sarnia or Collingwood on Lake Huron, thence by steamer to Thunder Bay
or Duluth on Lake Superior, and thence by rail to Winnipeg. The journey by the former route is quicker by
about a day, but the latter is more economical. By either
of these routes the settler will be met by the agents of
American land and railway companies, who will endeavour to persuade settlement in the United States as
preferable to Canada; but the settler is advised to proceed
direct to his intended destination, and decide upon his
location after personal inspection. It may be added that
most of the rivers and lakes in Manitoba and the north-
west are navigable, and that steamers now ply during
the season on the river Saskatchewan between Winnipeg
and Edmonton, a distance by water of about 1200.
miles, with passengers and freight, calling at Prince
Albert, Carlton, Battleford, and other places on the way.
Steamers also run regularly between Winnipeg, St. Vincent, and other places on the Red River. There is also
steam communication on the river Assiniboine between
Fort Ellice and Winnipeg.

11. **Canadian Pacific Railway.**—This line of railway, which is to connect the Atlantic and Pacific oceans, is now in course of construction by the Canadian Pacific Railway Company, and is expected to cost from 75 to 80 millions of dollars. A thousand miles of the line are now in operation, and it is expected in 1883 to reach the Rocky Mountains.

12. **Climate.**—Manitoba is situated in the middle of the continent, nearly equidistant from the pole and the equator, and the Atlantic and Pacific oceans. The climate gives conditions of decided heat in summer and decided cold in winter. The snow goes away, and ploughing begins in April, which is about the same time as in the older provinces of Canada and the Northern United States on the Atlantic seaboard, and the North-western States of Minnesota and Wisconsin. The crops are harvested in August. The long sunny days of summer bring vegetation of all sorts to rapid maturity. The days are warm and the nights cool. Autumn begins about the 20th of September and lasts till November, when the regular frosts set in. The winter proper comprises part of November, December, January, February, and March. Spring comes early in April. The summer months are part of May, June, July, August, and part of September. In winter the thermometer sinks to 30 and sometimes 40 degrees below zero, but this degree of cold in the dry atmosphere of the north-west does not produce any unpleasant sensations. The weather is not felt to be colder than in the province of Quebec, nor so cold as milder winters in climates where the frost, or even a less degree of cold than frost, is accompanied with damp or wind. The testimony is universal on this point. Snow does not fall on the prairies to an average greater depth than 18 inches, and buffaloes and horses graze out of doors all winter. They scratch the snow off the prairie, and grow fat upon the grass they find beneath it. Horned cattle also graze out of doors part of the winter, but in some states of the weather they require to be brought in. Instances are, however, stated in which horned cattle have grazed out all the winter.

13. **Soil.**—The soil is a deep alluvial deposit of unsurpassed richness. It is mostly prairie, and covered with grass. It produces bountiful crops of cereals, grasses, roots, and vegetables. So rich is the soil that wheat has been cropped off the same place for forty years without manure, and without showing signs of exhaustion. The following extracts from the reports of the English and Scotch farmers selected by the farmers in their respective districts who went out to Canada in 1879, to report upon the country, are interesting and reliable on this subject:—

Mr. BIGGAR, The Grange, Dalbeattie.

" As a field for wheat raising, I would much prefer Manitoba to Dakota. The first cost of the land is less, the soil is deeper and will stand more cropping, the sample of wheat is better, and the produce 5 to 10 bushels per acre more, all of which is profit."

Mr. GEORGE COWAN, Annan,

speaking of Mr. Mackenzie's farm at Burnside, says :—
" I was certainly surprised at the wonderful fertility of the soil, which is a rich black loam, averaging about 18 inches of surface soil, on friable clay subsoil, 5 and 6 feet in depth, beneath which is a thin layer of sand, lying on a stiff clay. The land is quite dry, and is well watered by a fine stream which flows through it."

*   *   *   *

" The land between Rapid City and the Assiniboine, which lies to the southward, 25 miles distant, is a nice loam with clay subsoil on top of gravel. I was very highly impressed with the fertility of the soil, some of it being, without exception, the richest I have ever seen, and I have little doubt it will continue for many years to produce excellent crops of grain without any manure, and with very little expense in cultivation."

Mr. JOHN LOGAN, Earlston, Berwick, says:—

" All the land round this district (Assiniboine) is very good, being four feet deep of black loam, as we saw from a sand-pit."

Mr. JOHN SNOW, Midlothian.

"We saw that a black vegetable mould covered the surface from 18 inches to two, three, or four feet deep."

Mr. JOHN MAXWELL, Carlisle.

"The soil throughout the country is a rich black loam, 6 inches to 6 feet deep, almost entirely free from stones, and varying in quality in different districts, on a subsoil of strong or friable clay or sand."

14.—Average Crops.—The average wheat yield in Manitoba and the North-West would appear to range from 20 to 30 bushels per acre, and the weight from 60lb. to 66lb. per bushel. Barley and oats yield good averages, as also potatoes and other root crops.

The following figures, taken from the reports of the delegates of the English and Scotch tenant farmers, may also be found interesting on this point :—

Mr. JAMES BIGGAR, of the Grange, Dalbeattie, says :—

"We heard very different statements of the yield of wheat, varying from 25 to 40 bushels. McLean, a farmer near Portage, had 1230 bushels of Fife wheat off 40 acres. Another man, a native of Ross-shire, who was ploughing his own land, told us he had cropped it for 17 years in succession, his last crop yielding 35 bushels per acre. Mr. Ryan, M.P., a good authority, said the average of wheat might safely be taken at 25 to 30 bushels, and of oats 60 bushels. . . . . Next day we drove over to Messrs. Riddles' farm ; their wheat has averaged fully 30 bushels per acre."

Mr. GEORGE COWAN, Glenluce, Wigtown, says :—

"Mr. Mackenzie's farm is at Burnside, about 9 miles from Portage la Prairie. . . . . He favoured me with his average for the seasons of 1877 and 1878, and his estimate for the present year. Wheat crop, 1877, 41 bushels ; 1878, 36 bushels ; this year (1879) he expects it to be close on 40 bushels ; average weight, 60 to 62lb. ; but he has grown it as high as 64 lb. per bushel. Oats last year (1878) he had a yield of 88 bushels from 2 bushels of seed sown on one acre; this year (1879) his estimate is from 75 to 80 bushels per acre. Mr. M. also grows excellent root crops, his swede turnips averaging 30 to 35 tons; and potatoes, without any care in cultivation, sometimes even not being moulded up, yield between 300 and 400 bushels of 60lb. Onions when cultivated are also very prolific, yielding as much as 300 bushels per acre. Mangold also grows very heavy crops, but I did not see any on the ground."

*   *   *   *

"We spent a short time on the farm of Mr. McBeth, and walked over a field which, I was informed, had been continuously under crop for 54 years. . . . . I was told it would average 28 or 30 bushels per acre."

All the other delegates confirm these figures.

15. Homestead Exemption Law.—In Manitoba a homestead exemption law was passed in 1872, which exempts from seizure for debt 160 acres of land, house, stables, barns, furniture, tools, farm implements in use, one cow, two oxen, one horse, four sheep, two pigs, and thirty days' provender for same.

(B) ONTARIO.

1. Free Grants of Land.—Every head of a family can obtain a free grant of 200 acres of land, and any person 18 years of age may obtain 100 acres in the free grant districts. The conditions are:—15 acres in each grant of 100 acres to be cleared and under crop in five years; a habitable house, at least 16 feet by 20, built; and residence on the land at least six months in each year. The patent is issued at the end of 5 years.

2. Price of Lands.—Uncleared lands can also be purchased at prices varying from 2s. to 40s. per acre. Cleared and improved farms with buildings can be bought at from £4 to £10 per acre. The money can nearly always be paid in instalments covering several years.

3. **Soil.**—The soil of the country varies in different localities, but a large proportion is of the very best description for agricultural purposes.

4. **Climate.**—The climate is much the same as in some other parts of the Dominion. Cereals, grasses, and roots produce large crops, and fruits grow in great abundance; hemp, tobacco, and sugar beet are also profitable crops; maize and tomatoes ripen well, and peaches and grapes come to perfection in the open air.

5. **Means of Communication.**—The province possesses excellent means of communication, both by railways and by water through the lakes, and the River St. Lawrence, with all parts of the Dominion and to the Atlantic ports.

6. **Education.**—The public schools are all free and non-sectarian. All resident children between the ages of 5 and 21 are allowed to attend them.

7. **Cities and Towns.**—There are several large cities and towns in this province; among others, Toronto, Ottawa, Hamilton, London, Kingston, etc.

8. **Minerals.**—In mineral wealth it has great resources, producing iron, copper, lead, silver, marble, petroleum, salt, etc. Its immense forests of pine timber are well known.

9. **Manufactures and Exports.**—Its principal manufactures are cloth, linen, clothing, leather, furniture, sawn timber, flax, iron and hardware, paper, soap, cotton and woollen goods, steam-engines and locomotives, wooden ware of all descriptions, agricultural implements, etc. Cattle, sheep, and pigs, dairy and agricultural produce are exported largely from this province, and the trade is increasing rapidly.

10. **Average Rate of Wages, Cost of Board, and House Rent in Ontario.**—*Toronto District:* Farm labourers, per day, without board, 3*s*. 6*d*. to 4*s*.; per week, with board, 12*s*. to 14*s*.; female farm servants, with board,

per month, 20s. to 25s.; general labourers, per day, 5s.; railway labourers, 5s. 6d.; masons, 10s.; bricklayers, 10s.; carpenters, 8s.; lumbermen, 6s.; shipwrights, 6s.; smiths, 6s.; wheelwrights, 6s.; gardeners, with board, 16s. per week; without board, 5s. per day; miners, 3s. to 4s.; mill hands, 5s. 6d.; saddlers, 6s.; bootmakers, 6s.; tailors, 6s.; female cooks, per month, £1 12s. to £2; domestic servants, £1 5s. to £1 10s.; laundresses, £1 12s. to £1 18s.; cost of board, 12s. per week; house rent from £1 to £1 12s. per month.

Ottawa District: Immigrant farm labourers obtained this year (1882) during harvest from £3 8s. to £5 8s. per month, without board; others were engaged at £2 16s. to £3 5s. per month, with board. Female farm servants are not employed for outdoor work in fields; general labourers, per day, 6s.; railway labourers, 5s. 6d. to 6s.; masons, 10s. (very few required); bricklayers, 10s. (very few required), carpenters, 6s. to 7s.; lumbermen, per month, with board, £3 15s. to £8 8s.; blacksmiths, £3 15s. to £5 5s.; wheelwrights, £3 15s. to £4 4s.; gardeners, £3 15s. to £4 4s.; miners, per day, 6s.; mill hands, 5s. to 8s.; saddlers, per week, without board, £1 8s. to £2 2s.; bootmakers and tailors can earn, on piecework, from £1 5s. to £2 2s. per week; female cooks, per month, £2 2s.; domestic servants, £1 5s. to £1 18s.; laundresses, £1 10s.; board, per week, 10s. to 14s.; house rent, 14s. to £1.

11. **Testimony in Favour of Ontario.**—Professor Sheldon, an eminent authority on agricultural questions, paid a visit to Canada a year or two ago, and has given the results of his observations in a small pamphlet. (See page 63.)

In the autumn of 1879 a number of tenant farmers, representing different districts of the United Kingdom, visited Canada, for the purpose of reporting upon its agricultural capabilities and resources to their friends at home. A few brief selections from their reports bearing on the Province of Ontario are as follows :—

MR. BIGGAR, The Grange, Dalbeattie.

" A great deal of Western Ontario would compare very

favourably with some parts of England. The land is good
and fairly managed; there is a nice proportion of timber,
and the farmers' houses are in many cases exceedingly neat
and comfortable. They have, in fact, an air of refinement
and prosperity beyond what we expected in a comparatively new country. We believe it would be hard to find
in any country of similar size so many men who have done
as well as Ontario farmers. Many who went out 30 or 40
years ago with nothing now own farms and stock worth
£2000 to £6000. There are, however, a good many who
have mortgages on their farms to a considerable amount,
for which they pay 7 to 8 per cent. interest. This, together with bad seasons and emigration to the north-west,
accounts for the large number of farms which are at present for sale. I may here remark that the custom of let-
ting land is not so common as in this country. Farms
are only let from year to year, and as the tenant in these
circumstances is supposed to take out what he can, owners
are more ready to sell than to let. At the same time, it
is possible to get farms on rent, and emigrants from this
country would do well to rent a farm for a year or two
until they have time to look round."

MR. THOMAS IRVING, Bowness.

"The Canadians loved their country; many old men
who came over to England with the intention of ending
their days went back again. They like the climate of
Ontario better than that of England. It was not usually
muggy out there, nor did it rain every day, but when it
did rain it came down heavy. He advised intending
emigrants to go to Ontario, where a state of things existed
much as at home; they would find good roads, good
schools, churches of all denominations, plenty of railway
communication—in fact, civilization was quite as far
advanced as at Bowness, if not more so. It would be
much better to pay a little more for land there than to go
1500 miles or so up the country, at the risk of being
unable to see a newspaper for twelve months."

MR. GEORGE WILKEN, Aberdeen.

"Went to the root show, London, Ontario, and it

surprised me more than all the others. Coming along I
had seen some good fields of swedes and mangolds, but
was not prepared to see swedes, mangolds, and potatoes
that would put any of our exhibits for this year far into
the shade. Mr. Stock was very hard on me for only allow-
ing they could beat us *this year.* Our next inspection was
fruits. Here I saw, and tasted too, fruit of every hue and
flavour. It will give some idea of the show of apples
when I mention that the varieties in sections varied from
six to forty-two, and all were such as I had never seen.
Peaches, grapes (all outdoor), melons, tomatoes, squash,
and ever so many kinds of fruit I never saw or heard of."

Mr. JAMES PALMER, Somersetshire.

"I am much pleased with Canada, for the prospects are
different to what they are in England, especially for
farmers. My sons are delighted with the country and the
farms. I have purchased for them in all 273 acres, in two
farms situated seven miles from this, near the main road
towards Exeter. They have a good house on each lot,
with orchards, out-buildings, etc., and 75 acres fenced and
under cultivation on each lot. The whole cost $7500—
less than I had to pay rent for land in two years in
Somersetshire—that is to say, two years' rent per acre. I
can strongly recommend this country to my friends and
others who intend to emigrate."

(C) QUEBEC.

1. **Free Grants of Land.**—Upon eight of the great
colonization roads, every male colonist and emigrant being
18 years of age may obtain a free grant of 100 acres. The
conditions are that at the end of the fourth year a dwell-
ing must have been erected on the land, and 12 acres be
under cultivation. Letters patent are then granted.
Crown lands can also be purchased at 30 cents to 60
cents an acre.

2. **Homestead Law.**—The province has a homestead law exempting from seizure, under certain conditions, the property of emigrants.

3. **Education.**—Primary education is compulsory. The cost is defrayed by the collection of small fees and by a liberal Government grant.

4. **The Soil and its Productions.**—The soil of the province is extremely rich, and susceptible of the highest cultivation. It is adapted for the growth of very varied products; cereals, hay, and green crops grow everywhere in abundance where the land is at all fairly tilled. Cattle breeding is being carried on on a very large scale, and within the past few years there have been exported from Quebec to Great Britain large quantities of dead meat and cattle, not excelled by the best English breeds. For pasturage the lands of Quebec are of special excellence. Those in the Eastern Townships and north of the Ottawa have special attractions for English settlers. The impulse given to agriculture by the active co-operation of the Government is working great benefit and leading to strides little dreamt of five years ago. The exports from the forest during the year 1881 amounted to $12,785,223, the agricultural produce to $8,242,024, and the export of animals and their produce reached the sum of $12,478,690.

5. **Agriculture and Colonization.**—The great bulk of the rural population live by agriculture. The extent of the farms generally is 100 acres; farms in the older settlements being worth as a rule from $2,000 to $4,000. The sons of farmers invariably push back into the new settlements, where a partially cleared farm may be purchased for about $200: or purchase a lot from the Crown lands at a cost of between 30 to 40 cents (1s. 3d. to 1s. 8d. sterling) per acre; or take a *free grant* along one of the colonization roads. There are five main centres of colonization :—*The Valley of the Saguenay*—The extent of land surveyed and disposable in this district is about 616,600 acres, the price of which is about 20 cents (10d. sterling) per acre. *The Valley of the St. Maurice*—There are in the townships of this district surveyed, divided into farm lots,

441,200 acres of land, for sale at 30 cents (1s. 3d. sterling)
per acre. *The Valley of the Ottawa*—The number of acres
surveyed and divided into farm lots actually to be disposed
of in this district is 1,358,500 acres, the price of which is
30 cents per acre. *The Eastern Townships*—In this rich
grazing district there are 922,300 acres of wild land,
which the Government is prepared to sell at a moderate
rate. The Government lands in this section sell at from
50 to 60 cents (2s. 1d. to 2s. 6d. sterling) per acre. The
Eastern Townships present more than ordinary attractions
to the agriculturist and capitalist from Great Britain.
Gaspe—In this district the Government offers for sale
491,900 acres of land, at the rate of 20 and 30 cents (10d.
to 1s. 3d. sterling) per acre. Besides this on the south
shore of the Lower St. Lawrence, the Government offers
for sale 1,432,200 acres, at 30 cents (1s. 3d. sterling)
per acre.

6. **Means of Communication.**—This is afforded by
railways and by the River St. Lawrence. This province
contains the two great ports of shipment, Montreal and
Quebec, both of which have extensive wharfage accommodation, and ocean-going vessels of 4000 tons can be
moored alongside the quays.

7. **Cities.**—The principal cities are Quebec and
Montreal, and there are many large towns.

8. **Mines and Fisheries.**—Gold, lead, silver, iron,
copper, platinum, etc., etc., are found,—but mining in this
province is only yet in its infancy. Phosphate mining is
becoming an important industry; its value as a fertilizer
is recognized in England and France, and large quantities
are being exported. The fisheries are abundant, and in
1876 the yield was of the value of $2,097,677.

9. **Average Rate of Wages, Cost of Board, and
House Rent in the Province of Quebec.**—Farm
labourers, per day, without board, 4s. to 6s.; per month,
and board, £3 to £5 10s.; female farm servants, £1 5s. to
£2 2s.; general labourers, per day, 4s. to 6s.; railway
labourers, 5s. to 6s.; masons, 6s. to 9s.; bricklayers, 6s. to

9*s.*; carpenters, 6*s.* to 9*s.*; lumberers, and board, 6*s.* to 8*s.*; shipwrights, per day, 6*s.* to 8*s.*; smiths, 6*s.* to 8*s.*; wheelwrights, 6*s.* to 8*s.*; gardeners, with board, per month, £4 to £5, without board, per day, 4*s.* to 6*s.*; miners, 6*s.* to 8*s.*; mill hands, 4*s.* to 6*s.*; engine drivers, 7*s.* to 10*s.*; saddlers, 8*s.* to 10*s.*; bootmakers, 5*s.* to 8*s.*; tailors, 4*s.* to 6*s.*; female cooks, per month, £1 12*s.* to £2 10*s.*; domestic servants, in great demand, £1 5*s.* to £2 2*s.*; laundresses per day, 3*s.* to 4*s.*; cost of board, per week, 12*s.* to 16*s.*; rent of mechanics' and labourers' dwellings, £1 5*s.* to £1 12*s.* per month.

(D) NEW BRUNSWICK.

1. **Free Grants of Land.**—A grant of 100 acres may be obtained by any person upon the following conditions: On payment of $20 cash to aid in construction of roads and hedges, or labour of the value of $10 per year for 3 years. A house to be built within 2 years. Ten acres to be cleared and cultivated in 3 years. Proof of residence on the land.

2. **Soil and Production.**—The soil is fertile, and produces all the fruits generally found in England. Wheat averages about 20, barley 29, oats 34, buckwheat 33, rye 20, Indian corn 41, potatoes 226, turnips 456 bushels to the acre. The potatoes and fruits command good prices in the English market.

3. **Manufactures.**—Shipbuilding is one of the staple industries of the province, but its manufacturies generally are increasing rapidly. There are manufactories of woollen and cotten goods, boots and shoes, leather, carriages, wooden ware, paper, soap, hardware, etc., etc.

4. **Climate.**—In New Brunswick the summer is warmer and the winter colder than in England, the ranges of temperature being in the interior from 92° above zero to 18° below zero (Fahrenheit); the whole number of days, however, in which the temperature is below zero rarely exceeds 20. It seldom happens that the mercury is below zero for 4 successive days. In general the winters are pleasant,

and a few days of extreme cold are nothing in comparison with the average amount of fine weather. People living in New Brunswick do not suffer more, if as much, from cold as those who live in Great Britain and other countries where the winters are more humid and the temperature less steady. All business is carried on as actively in winter as in summer, and the people do not wear more nor different clothing than that worn in England and the rest of northern Europe.

5. **Average Rate of Wages, Cost of Board, and House Rent in New Brunswick.**—Farm labourers, per day, without board, 3*s.* 6*d.* to 4*s.*; per week and board, 12*s.* 6*d.* to 14*s.* 6*d.*; female farm servants, per month and board, 18*s.* 6*d.* to £1 5*s.*; general labourers, per day, 5*s.* 6*d.* to 8*s.*; railway labourers, 4*s.* to 5*s.*; masons, 9*s.* to 10*s.*; bricklayers, 11*s.* to 12*s.* 6*d.*; carpenters, 5*s.* 6*d.* to 8*s.*; lumbermen, per month, with board, £3 5*s.* to £4 16*s.* (none employed otherwise); shipwrights, 6*s.* to 7*s.*; smiths, 6*s.* to 6*s.* 6*d.*; wheelwrights, 8*s.* to 12*s.* 6*d.*; gardeners, with board, per week, £1 12*s.* to £2; without board, per day, 4*s.* to 4*s.* 6*d.*; miners, 3*s.* to 3*s.* 6*d.*; mill hands, 5*s.* to 6*s.* 6*d.*; engine drivers, per month, £7 5*s.* to £13 (average, £12); saddlers, per day, 4*s.* to 6*s.*; bootmakers, 5*s.* to 8*s.*; tailors, 6*s.* to 8*s.*; female cooks, per month, £1 12*s.* to £2 10*s.*; domestic servants, £1 5*s.* to £1 12*s.*; laundresses, per week, 12*s.* 6*d.* to 16*s.* 6*d.*; cost of board, per week, varying, 12*s.* to £1; rent of labourers' dwellings, per annum £6 to £7 5*s.*, per month 12*s.*

(E) NOVA SCOTIA.

1. **Land.**—The quantity of land for disposal in this province is limited. The price is $44 per 100 acres (about £9), free grants, however, being given to *bonâ fide* settlers.

2. **Soil.**—The soil produces good crops of cereals and roots, and large quantities of apples are grown for export. Wheat averages, per acre, 18 bushels; rye, 21 bushels;

barley, 35 bushels; oats, 34 bushels; buckwheat, 33 bushels; Indian corn (maize), 42 bushels; turnips, 420 bushels; potatoes, 250 bushels; mangel wurzel, 500 bushels; beans, 22 bushels; hay, 2 tons.

3. **Fisheries.**—The fisheries of Nova Scotia are an important interest for that province. In 1881, the number of vessels employed was 647, number of boats 11,919, and number of men, 27,526. The quantity of codfish caught was 583,029 cwt., of mackerel, 63,377 barrels; of haddock, 116,160 cwt.; of herrings, 198,269 barrels; of lobsters, 4,895,692 cans. Of fish oils, the quantity obtained was 417,022 gallons. The total value of the fisheries of this province for 1881 was $6,214,775.

4. **Minerals.**—Gold, iron, coal, and gypsum are found in large quantities.

5. **Education,** which is very general, is partly supported by direct taxation, supplemented by liberal annual grants from the Legislature, which in 1880 amounted to about $169,000. The total expenditure for public schools in that year was $557,765. At the common schools, which are subject to the control of the Government, the average number of scholars in daily attendance had been estimated at 100,000, and all are free.

6. **Railways.**—There are several railways in the province, giving it communication with other parts of Canada. Halifax, which is the chief city of the province, is the winter port of the Dominion. It possesses a fine harbour, and is connected by railways with all parts of the continent.

7. **Average Rate of Wages, Cost of Board, and House Rent in Nova Scotia.**—Farm labourers, per day, without board, 4s. 6d.; per month, and board, £3 5s. to £4 4s.; female farm servants, 16s. to 25s.; general labourers, per day, 4s. to 5s.; railway labourers, 4s. to 5s.; boiler makers, 8s.; masons, 10s.; bricklayers, 10s.; carpenters, 6s.; lumbermen, 6s.; shipwrights, 10s.; smiths, 8s.; wheelwrights, 6s. 6d. to 12s.; gardeners, per month, with board, £3 15s. to £6; per month, without board, £5 5s. to £8; miners, 5s. to 6s.; mill hands, per day, 4s. 6d.

to 5*s.*; engine drivers, 7*s.* to 9*s.*; saddlers, per week, £1 5*s.*
to £2; bootmakers, per day, 5*s.*; tailors, per week, £2 5*s.*
to £2 10*s.*; cost of board, per week, 12*s.* 6*d.* to 14*s.* 6*d.*;
house rent, per year, £3 to £5.

(F) PRINCE EDWARD ISLAND.

Price of Lands.—Most of the lands in this province
are taken up, but improved farms can be obtained from
about £4 per acre. This island produces excellent crops
of cereals, and is noted for the good quality of its oats.
Horses, cattle, and sheep are plentiful, and the country is
exceedingly well spoken of as regards the fertility of the
soil and its cheapness. .

(G) BRITISH COLUMBIA.

1. General Description.—This province, which includes Vancouver's Island, is the most western of the
provinces which constitute the Dominion of Canada, its
boundaries being the Rocky Mountains on the east, and
the Pacific Ocean on the west. It possesses many fine
harbours, one of which (Burrard Inlet) will probably form
the terminus of the Canadian Pacific Railway when completed; 125 miles of the line in this province are now
under contract.

2. Land.—Heads of families, widows, or single men
can obtain free grants of land from 160 to 320 acres,
according to locality; the fee is about $7. Surveyed
lands can be purchased at $1 per acre, payable over two
years, and improved farms cost from £1 to £8 per acre.
British Columbia has a large extent of valuable timber
land, productive fisheries, which are increasing in value
yearly; gold and coal are also found in large quantities.
The yield of gold, from 1858 to 1880, was equal to about
forty-five millions of dollars.

CHAPTER IV.

THE CHURCH AND EDUCATION IN CANADA.

1. **Ecclesiastical Information.**—There is no Established Church in Canada—all denominational Christians are upon an equality, the Government only interfering in the matter of secular education. For ecclesiastical purposes the continent has been divided out into the following 17 Dioceses, viz:—Fredericton, Nova Scotia, Quebec, Toronto, Newfoundland, Montreal, Huron, Ontario, Algoma, Niagara, Rupert's Land, Saskatchewan, Moosonee, Athabasca, Columbia, Caledonia, and New Westminster.

Each diocese has its bishop and a large staff of clergy. Whenever a church is wanted, the bishop or the nearest clergyman should be written to, and they will no doubt co-operate with the inhabitants of the place in the erection of one.

At all events, the services of the clergy can always be obtained for the baptism of your children, for marriages and burials, and from time to time for the administration of Holy Communion, and the Bishops hold frequent Confirmations.

2. **The System of Education.**—In Ontario, the system of education is free and compulsory in the public or common schools, and pupils have opportunities for acquiring a good substantial course of instruction, and for passing to the grammar or high schools and colleges on easy terms.

In Quebec and the Maritime Provinces education is conducted on broad principles also.

In Manitoba and the North-West Territory the land is surveyed into districts of six miles square, containing in all thirty-six sections of a mile square each ; two of these sections in every district are reserved by the Government to be sold to provide funds for the establishment of schools as they may be required, and education is also assisted from time to time by grants of public money, irrespective of religious questions.

In every village springing up facilities will be found for free education, and no persons need fear any difficulty in providing for the education of their families.

There is a university, modelled on that of London, in Manitoba, open to those who wish to obtain a higher class of education than is found in the ordinary free schools.

3. **The Church of England Settlers' Society of the Diocese of Rupert's Land** for settlers in Manitoba and the North-West.

This Society has just been formed, and its "objects" are commended to the attention of all persons proposing to settle in this part of Canada.

Article II. of the Constitution declares these objects to be as follow :—

To invite each settler in the North-West, being or desiring to become a member of the Church of England, to place himself, immediately on his arrival in this province, in communication with the officers of the society, who will give him :—

I. Advice and information on any subject connected with his settlement in the country.

II. References to reliable persons in any quarter of the North-West which he may desire to visit.

III. Letters of introduction to the clergymen of the Church stationed in any part of the North-West.

IV. Facilities in obtaining the services and ordinances of the Church; as by furnishing him and his family with seats in church; and by supplying them with introductions to the clergymen in charge.

V. Countenance, and in every way treat him as a brother Churchman, and exhibit to him and his family all possible kindness.

The residences or places of business of the officers are given below, and these gentlemen, with the ladies of their families, will at all times be happy to carry out these objects on their parts. It is hoped that every settler, whatever may be his position in life, will encourage the operations of the Society by a frank and free acceptance of the friendly offices hereby tendered. Settlers are invited to communicate with the officers personally, if possible, or if this be inconvenient, by letter.

THE FOLLOWING ARE THE OFFICERS :—

Patron.—The Most Reverend the Bishop of Rupert's Land, and Metropolitan, Bishop's Court, Winnipeg.
President.—George B. Spencer, Collector of Customs, Winnipeg.

COUNCIL.

Winnipeg.—The Very Rev. Dean Grisdale, B.D.; the Ven. Archdeacon Pinkham, B.D.; Rev. Canon O'Meara, M.A.; Rev. Canon Matheson, B.D.; Rev. O. Fortin, B.A., Rector of Holy Trinity; Rev. E. S. Pentreutb Incumbent of Christ Church; Rev. A. Stunden, B.A., Assistant, Holy Trinity; Rev. H. T. Leslie, B.A.; Rev. A. E. Cowley, Rector of St. James'; the Hon. the Chief Justice of Manitoba; the Hon. John Norquay, Premier of the Province; the Hon. D. M. Walker, Attorney-General; the Hon. Mr. Justice Miller; R. H. Hunter, Manager, Imperial Bank; Amos Rowe, Proprietor *Times;* Alexander Logan, Mayor; Donald Codd, Inspector, Dominion Lands.
St. Andrew's.—Rev. R. Young, B.A., Incumbent; Captain Kennedy, J.P.; T. Truthwaite.
Pembina Crossing.—Charles Selwyn.
Springfield.—Rev. S. Pritchard, Incumbent;—Oldfield, William Corbett.
Cook's Creek.—James Fullerton.
Millbrook.—George Eadie.
Plympton.— — Lewis.
Clear Springs.—John Lund.
Dynevor.—Ven. Archdeacon Cowley, B.D.; Rev. B. McKenzie, Incumbent of St. Peter's; W. Pruden; A. H. Vaughan.
St. Paul.—Samuel James.
St. James.—P. Bruce.
Headingly.—Hon. W. Tait; J. Cameron.
High Bluff.—Rev. Mark Jukes, Incumbent of St. Margaret's; J. A. K. Drummond, M.P.P.; A. Spence, J.P.
Portage la Prairie.—Rev. A. L. Fortin, Incumbent of St. Mary's; W. J. Pratt.
Millford.—G. S. Newcombe; Major Rogers.
Westbourne.—Rev. Thomas Cook, Incumbent; A. E. Smalley, J.P.
Emerson.—Rev. C. J. Brenton, M.A., Incumbent of St. Luke's Church; J. E. Cooper; Captain Nash, County Registrar; J. Carman.
Victoria.—J. Vincent, J.P.; W. Vincent.
Mapleton.—Rev. N. C. Martin, Incumbent of St. Clement's.
Morris.—Rev. A. G. Pinkham, Incumbent of All Saints'; S. J Collum; H. Hall.
Nelsonville.—Rev. T. N. Wilson, Missionary; George Leary.

E

Rapid City.—Rev. J. P. Sargent, B.A., Incumbent; Rev. W. O. Bruneau, Sioux Mission; Rev. G, Turnbull; G. Lindsay; W. Thompson.

Brandon.—Rev. J. Boydell, M.A., Incumbent; Rev. C. B. Dundas, B.A.; Rev. C. T. Weatherley, Pultney; A. Jukes, Manager, Imperial Bank; T. M. Daly, Jun., Barrister; Richmond Spencer, M.D.; J. W Willis, Banker; George E. Fortier; Eustace Bucke.

Stonewall.—Rev. W. F. Green, Curate in Charge.

Derford Point.—Rev. George Aitkens, B.A., Missionary.

Fairford.—Rev. George Bruce.

Touchwood Hills.—Rev. Gilbert Cook.

Fort Frances.—Rev. Robert Phair, Alberton.

Keematin.—Rev. J. Render, Devon; Rev. B. Spence, Islington; Rev. J. Irvine, Lac Seul.

Stodderville.—W. Winram, M.P.P.

Birtle.—Lawrence Herchmer.

Shell River.—Col. Boulton.

Holland P.O.—Conway Dobbs.

Beaconsfield.—John Hall; J. Ashby.

EXECUTIVE COMMITTEE.

Winnipeg.—Rev. Canon O'Meara, M.A., St. John's College; Dean Grisdale, B.D.,·St. John's College; Rev. Canon Matheson, B.D., St. John's College; Rev. S. Pritchard; Rev. O. Fortin, B.A., Holy Trinity; Ven. Archdeacon Pinkham, B.D., Superintendent of Education; Hon. C. Inkster, Sheriff of the Province; W. G. Fonseca, Broker; G. F. Carruthers, Broker; J. H. Brock, Broker; A. H. Whitcher, Dominion Land Agent; W. R. Nursey, Provincial Auditor, Government Offices; J. H. Rowan, Engineer, C.P.R.; S. Mulvey, Collector Inland Revenue; George P. Black, Canadian Pacific Railway; Palmer Clarke; Captain Howard.

St. James.—R. Tait, J.P.

Stoney Mountain.—S. L. Bedson, Warden Provincial Penitentiary.

SECRETARY-TREASURER.

Winnipeg.—William Leggo, Master in Equity.

ASSISTANT SECRETARY.

Winnipeg.—G. Byron Philip, Barrister.

CORRESPONDING SECRETARY.

Brandon.—Loftus M. Fortier, Commission Merchant.

CLERICAL AGENTS IN LIVERPOOL. ·

Rev. J. Bridger and Rev. R. O. Greep, St. Nicholas' Parish Church.

Settlers can .obtain all information at the office of W. G. Fonseca, Esq., No. 495, Main Street, Winnipeg.

4. ONTARIO AGRICULTURAL COLLEGE.

Applications are often received on behalf of young gentlemen who desire to fit themselves for agricultural work, but who are without any experience. There are three courses open to such persons. 1. To undergo a course of instruction at the Ontario Agricultural College. A matriculation examination in elementary subjects has to be passed. Candidates must not be less than fifteen years of age. The fee is £10 per year. Pupils pay their own board and lodging, which is not expensive. They are paid for their labour on the college farm, which materially lightens the cost of maintenance. Only a hundred members can actually reside in the college, but pupils who cannot be accommodated, board out under supervision. They acquire a practical as well as a theoretical knowledge of agriculture. The terms commence in April and October in each year. Communications respecting admission, etc., should be addressed to the President, Ontario Agricultural College, Guelph, Canada. 2. To hire themselves out to farmers for their board until they are sufficiently competent to earn wages. 3. To take advantage of some of the proposals before the public from firms who profess to be able to place young men in such positions, and to ensure their receiving a proper training on payment of a premium. This plan is however to be received with caution. In all these cases, however, great care is required to decide whether the young men are suited to the life that is proposed. Hard work is necessary, and very often rough fare compared with that to which they have been accustomed, and their mode of living is entirely altered. Many persons have gone out in such circumstances and have done well, but there are others who have failed, because they have not properly understood the sort of life they would have to lead.

CHAPTER V.

COST OF PASSAGE TO CANADA AND GENERAL INFORMATION.

1. Rates of Passage.—The following are the rates of passage from Liverpool, London, Glasgow, or Londonderry, to Quebec or Halifax:—

Saloon, £12 to £18. Intermediate, £8 8s. Government assisted steerage passages as under :—

1. For mechanics, navvies, general labourers and their families, per adult, £4; children between 12 and 1, £2; infants under 12 months, 10s.

2. For agricultural labourers and their families, per adult, £3; children between 12 and 1, £2; infants under 12 months, 10s.

3. For female domestic servants, £3.

Domestic servants are forwarded free of cost from the port of landing to any place in the provinces of Quebec or Ontario to which they may desire to proceed, or at which employment may be found for them. The other classes of emigrants have to pay their own railway fares in Canada.

The advertisements of the companies running steamers to Canada will be found in all the daily papers.

Settlers can go to Winnipeg by the all-rail route, or by way of the lakes; the latter is the most economical, but takes a day or two longer.

2. Offices of the Dominion of Canada in Great Britain :—

LONDON.—Sir Alexander T. Galt, G.C.M.G., etc., High Commissioner for the Dominion, 9, Victoria Chambers, London, S.W. Mr. Joseph Colmer, Secretary.

3. Agents of the Canadian Government in Canada :-

OTTAWA.—Mr. W. J. Wills, St. Lawrence and Ottawa Railway Station, Ottawa, Ontario.

TORONTO.—Mr. J. A. Donaldson, Strachan Avenue, Toronto, Ontario.

MONTREAL.—Mr. J. J. Daley, Montreal, Province of Quebec.
KINGSTON.—Mr. R. Macpherson, William Street, Kingston.
HAMILTON.—Mr. John Smith, Great Western Railway Station, Hamilton.
LONDON.—Mr. A. G. Smythe, London, Ontario.
HALIFAX.- Mr. E. Clay, Halifax, Nova Scotia.
ST. JOHN.—Mr. S. Gardner, St. John, New Brunswick.
QUEBEC.—Mr. L. Stafford, Point Levis, Quebec.
DULUTH (Minnesota).—Mr. McGovern.
WINNIPEG.—Mr. W. B. C. Grahame, Winnipeg, Manitoba.
DUFFERIN.—Mr. J. E. Tétu, Dufferin, Manitoba.
BRANDON.—Mr. Thomas Bennett, Brandon, Manitoba.

These officers will afford the fullest advice and protection. They should be immediately applied to on arrival. All complaints should be addressed to them. They will also furnish information as to lands open for settlement in their respective provinces and districts, farms for sale, demand for employment, rates of wages, routes of travel, distances, expenses of conveyance; and will receive and forward letters and remittances for settlers, etc., etc.

Clergy of Waterside Parishes Working on behalf of Emigrants.

Port of Liverpool.—Rev. J. Bridger, Rev. R. O. Greep, St. Nicholas' Church.
Port of London.—Royal Victoria and Albert Docks: St. Luke's and St. Matthew's, Rev. J. O. Bagdon. East India and West India and Millwall Docks: St. Luke's, Millwall, Rev. J. Hewlett, Vicarage; Rev. F. Hasloch, Alpha Road.
Gravesend.—Holy Trinity: Rev. Canon Scarth, Vicarage; Rev. F. C. Naish, 9, The Terrace; Rev. Anton Tien. 1, Cumberland Terrace. Tilbury Parochial Mission for Dock and Railway: Rev. F. C. Naish, Missionary Curate; Rev. A. E. Clementi-Smith, Rector. *Many Emigrants embark from Tilbury Station.*
Plymouth.—Holy Trinity: Rev. F. Barnes, Holy Trinity Vicarage, Hoe Street.
Bristol.—Rev. C. W. Holland, Shirehampton, Bristol.
Southampton.—Rev. C. D. Kebbell. St. James'.
Barrow-in-Furness.—Rev. A. B. Crosse, St. George's.
Hull.—Rev. S. Allwood, Mariners' Church.
Glasgow.—Rev. J. C. Brooke, Wellfield House, Springburn, Glasgow.
Greenock.—Rev. J. Trew, 61, Union Street, Greenock.
Londonderry.—Rev. F. L. Riggs, 33, Clarendon Street, Derry

Queenstown.—Rev. W. Daunt.
Sligo.—Rev. T. Heany.
London.—Rev. W. Panckridge, St. Matthew's, City Road; Rev. Dr.
Ross, St. Philip's, Stepney, E.; Rev. A. Styleman Herring, St. Paul's,
Clerkenwell; Rev. R. C. Billing, The Rectory, Spitalfields; Rev. J. H.
Bodily, St. Mark's, Silvertown, London Docks; Rev. C. W. T. Roberts,
Gothic House, St. Ann's Road, Stamford Hill, N.; Rev. Charles Bull,
St. John's, North Woolwich.

Clergy and others in America Working on behalf of Emigrants.
New York. — Rev. Cornelius L. Twing, 66, Cooper Avenue,
Brooklyn, E.D.
Manitoba.—Emerson: Rev. C. J. Brenton. Winnipeg: Very Rev.
Dean Grisdale, Archdeacon Pinkham, and all the Clergy; W. Leggo,
Esq. Rapid City: Rev. J. P. Sargent. Brandon: Rev. J. Boydell,
L. M. Fortier, Esq.

(Clergy and others are also recommended to write to W. Leggo, Esq.,
the Secretary-Treasurer of the Church of England Settlers' Society,
Winnipeg, Manitoba, Canada.)

Quebec.—Rev. M. M. Fothergill.
Montreal.—Rev. R. Lindsay, 278, Dorchester Street.

ORGANIZING AND GENERAL SECRETARY:
Rev. J. Bridger, St. Nicholas' Church, Liverpool,
Who will answer, as far as possible, inquiries addressed to him by
intending Emigrants, or by Clergy and others on their behalf.

CHAPTER VI.

SIMPLE HINTS FOR PRESERVING HEALTH.

1. **The Ventilation of your House.**—Plenty of fresh
air is necessary for the proper action of the lungs and for
the blood. Ventilation means the art of supplying fresh
air without draughts. If you have only one room, always
open the window and air the room well before going to
bed, particularly if you have been smoking. During the
greater part of the year the window may be a little open
all night if you have the means to give yourself and wife
and children plenty of clothes, but do not let the air blow

upon you. If you feel the draught too much with the window open at the top, nail a piece of wood, placed slantingly, along the top of the window and reaching three or four inches above it; open the window about one or two inches, and the air will strike against the slanting piece of wood as it enters, and be directed towards the ceiling and will not be felt. If you have any fireplace which you do not use in the summer, never stop it up; the chimney is a good ventilator; also, never close the regulator if you have one in a grate.

2. **Cleanliness of your Rooms.**—The air of a room can never be pure if the room is dirty. Uncarpeted rooms should be carefully swept every day, but not washed too often, as wood or bricks both absorb and retain water for some time, and make the air damp and cold. Wash in warm, dry weather, when the windows can be fully opened. The greatest impurity is, however, often given by the bed or furniture. Take great care that these are wiped and kept clean; all the bedclothes and mattress should be fully exposed to the air for an hour every morning, and the blankets should be shaken.

3. **Cleanliness and Dryness about your House.**— Do not allow any heaps of refuse to remain near the house; the air cannot be pure if these are constantly adding effluvia to it. The dust-bin is often badly placed in houses, and is too seldom emptied. Potato-parings, pea-husks, and remains of food, should either be burnt or put by for the pig or chickens. All the dirty house-water should be put on the garden, and not allowed to soak under the house, as too often happens. This water contains organic substances which are fertilizing, and the remains of the soap used in the house is also very good for vegetables. It a butt can be obtained and the dirty water poured into it, the garden could be watered from time to time. Take care that the rain from the roof does not soak under the house, or cause dampness of the walls.

4. **Hints on the Water you Use.**—If you have to fetch water from a distance and to store it in your house, never keep it in buckets or open pans. It is sure to get

foul; dust falls into it, and it will absorb substances from the air. Wood also gets soft, and may make the water impure. Put it into glazed earthenware or stoneware jars with covers—these jars are cheap and strong—every now and then throw out all the water, and wipe the inside of the jars with a clean cloth. If the water is from a surface stream or shallow well, it is probably a soft water, and will act on metals. In that case do not use metallic vessels more than you can help. Use iron vessels for cooking, and if they require mending, take care they are not mended with lead solder, which the water can dissolve. Many cases of lead poisoning have occurred from this solder being used. With such a soft surface-water do not even use zinc pails, but draw it in wooden buckets and store in stoneware jars.

5. **How to Make a Filter.**—The filtration of water is not difficult, even if you cannot afford to buy a regular filter. A simple filter can be made as follows:—Get a common earthenware garden flower-pot; cover the hole with a bit of zinc gauze, or a bit of clean-washed flannel, which should be changed from time to time; then get some rather small gravel, wash it very well, and put it into the pot to the height of 3 in.; then get some white sand and wash it very clean, and put that on the gravel to the height of 3 in.; then buy 2 lb. of animal charcoal, wash that also by putting it into a jug and pouring boiling water on it; then, when the charcoal has subsided, pour off the water, and put some more on for three or four times. When the charcoal has been well washed, put it on the sand and press it well down. Have 4 in. of charcoal, if possible. The filter is now ready, pour water into the pot, and let it run through the hole into a large glass bottle. After a time the charcoal will get clogged, or foul. Take off a little from the top and boil it two or three times, and then spread it out and let it dry before the fire. It will then be as good as ever. If you have a rain-water tank, always filter the rain-water before using it for drink or cooking, as rain-water often is collected from dirty roofs or becomes impure in the tank.

6. What to Drink.—If you wish to keep good health to old age, never touch spirits. Nothing can be better, both for you and· your family, than skimmed milk at dinner and supper. It is well always to boil it, and a little sugar makes it still more agreeable. When you have had any heavy work to do, do not take either beer, cider, or spirits. By far the best drink is thin oatmeal and water with a little sugar. The proportions are a $\frac{1}{4}$ lb. of oatmeal to two or three quarts of water, according to the heat of the day and your work and thirst; it should be well boiled, and then an ounce or $1\frac{1}{4}$ ounce of brown sugar added. If you find it thicker than you like, add three quarts of water. Before you drink it, shake up the oatmeal well through the liquid. In summer, drink this cold; in winter, hot. You will find it not only quenches thirst, but will give you more strength and endurance than any other drink. If you cannot boil it, you can take a little oatmeal mixed with cold water and sugar, but this is not so good; always boil it if you can. If at any time you have to make a very long day, as in harvest, and cannot stop for meals, increase the oatmeal to $\frac{1}{2}$ lb., or even $\frac{3}{4}$ lb., and the water to three quarts, if you are likely to be very thirsty. If you cannot get oatmeal, wheat flour will do, but not quite so well. It is quite a mistake to suppose spirits give strength; they give a spurt to a man, but that goes off, and if more than a certain quantity is taken they lessen the power of work.

7. Food.—Many kinds of vegetable food, oatmeal, maize, peas, and beans contain almost as much flesh-forming food as meat, and, when properly cooked, form a wholesome and agreeable substitute for it. Extravagance might be avoided and much more pleasure found in food if trouble were taken to learn how to cook some of these simple things.

8. Closets.—One of the best kinds of closet is an earth-closet. As good an earth-closet for a cottage as any, is simply a zinc bucket coming up close to the wood of the seat, and with a handle to enable it to be lifted out. The wooden top of the seat should be made with a hinge, so that it can be lifted up and the bucket removed and emptied from time to time. Very little earth is necessary if no slops are thrown into the bucket, and the earth can be thrown in with a shovel. It should be quite dry. In the winter time it should be dried under the fire before it is used. The material from an earth-closet may be put into a hole in the garden, and afterwards dug in as manure. All places of this kind, as well as water-closets, require attention and give a little trouble; but he must be the most careless of mortals who, in a matter so important for health, will not give half an hour's work every week to preserve cleanliness, and really no more time is demanded than this.

APPENDIX A.

COMMENDATORY LETTER.

REVEREND AND DEAR SIR,

I desire herewith to commend to your pastoral care and brotherly good offices,_____
from the Parish of_____ in the Diocese of_____
who is about to settle in_____

And I certify that_____
_____

Dated this_____

It is suggested that any clergyman giving a letter commendatory to a parishioner should copy out the letter in his own hand, in preference to using a printed form; and his letter would probably be still more valued, and likely to be more useful, if it could be written on the back of a photograph of the parish church or the cathedral of the diocese, or have such a photograph appended to it.

APPENDIX B.

PRAYERS FOR THE USE OF EMIGRANTS.

MORNING PRAYER.

In the Name of the Father, and of the Son, and of the Holy Ghost. Amen.

Lord, help me to pray.

Most gracious and merciful God, I worship Thee with the lowliest humility of my soul and body. All thanks and praise be to Thee for the safety, rest, and refreshment of the past night, and for the renewed life of another day. Blessed above all be Thy Holy Name for Thy promises of forgiveness and salvation, of grace and goodness in Jesus Christ. Fulfil these promises to me this day, I most humbly beseech Thee.

Deal not with me according to my iniquities, but be merciful unto me, and save me from the guilt and power of sin. Give me true faith in the Lord Jesus, and peace and joy in believing.

Let Thy Holy Spirit dwell within me, as the Spirit of wisdom and understanding, the Spirit of counsel and ghostly strength, the Spirit of knowledge and true godliness.

Bless me, O gracious God, in my calling, and enable me to do my duty faithfully in whatever work Thou shalt be pleased to employ me. Be nigh at hand to preserve me in all dangers and temptations. Support and comfort me under every anxiety, care, and sorrow. Provide for all my necessities, whether of body or soul.

May I remember Thee all the day, and ever speak and act as in Thy sight. Help me to be holy and righteous, charitable and humble, cheerful and contented. Let my condition be blessed and my behaviour useful to my neighbours and pleasing to Thee.

Bless all my dear friends and relations, especially

[   ]. Comfort and relieve the sick, and sorrowful, the needy, and him that hath no helper. Let Thy mercy descend upon the whole Church, especially upon that part of it to which I belong. Prosper the country in which I dwell; and let Thy mercy and goodness extend to all nations. Hear me, O Lord, in these my prayers and thanksgivings, and answer me according to Thy wisdom and love, for the sake of Jesus Christ our Saviour. Amen.

Our Father, which art in heaven, Hallowed be Thy Name. Thy kingdom come. Thy will be done in earth, As it is in heaven. Give us this day our daily bread. And forgive us our trespasses, As we forgive them that trespass against us. And lead us not into temptation; But deliver us from evil: For thine is the kingdom, The power, and the glory, For ever and ever. Amen.

The grace of our Lord Jesus Christ, and the love of God, and the fellowship of the Holy Ghost, be with us all evermore. Amen.

EVENING PRAYER.

Lord, help me to pray.

Almighty and most merciful God, in Thee we live and move and have our being. Thou, in Thy love, openest Thy hand and satisfiest the desires of all things living.

Through Thy undeserved goodness, I have been preserved in body and soul through another day. Glory and honour be to Thee for all the blessings of providence and grace which Thou hast bestowed upon me from morning until evening.

I am not worthy of the least of all Thy mercies; for my sins cry out against me. O that I may be truly and deeply sensible of them, and may confess them humbly and sorrowfully! I have this day fallen short in my duty to Thee and my neighbour. I have in many things offended against Thy holy law. All my negligences and ignorances; all my faults and sins are before Thee. Have mercy upon me, O God, for against Thee have I sinned and done all this evil in Thy sight.

Give me tenderness of conscience, and produce in me unfeigned repentance. I would plead Thy promises of forgiveness, I would put my whole trust in Thy mercy in Christ Jesus. For His sake pardon my iniquity, for it is great. May His precious blood, which cleanseth from all sin, be effectual for the washing away of my iniquities. Through His merits may I enjoy peace of conscience and peace with Thee, now that I am about to lie down and take my rest.

Thou hast brought me another day onward in my life, and I am one day nearer to the end. Teach me to number my days, that I may apply my heart unto wisdom. Keep me ever mindful of the solemn account I must ere long give before the judgment-seat of Christ. O that, whenever the hour of my death comes, I may fall asleep in Jesus! May my body be laid in its bed of darkness in hope of a glorious resurrection, and may my soul pass to the regions of light, and live with Thee in undying holiness and happiness.

Lord, I am unworthy to ask any petitions for myself or for others; yet I would humbly beseech Thee to hear me as for myself, so also for all whom I love; for all who have ever done me good; yea, even for all mine enemies. The wants of every creature are known to Thee; supply those wants, I heartily pray Thee, according to Thy power and wisdom and goodness.

Preserve me while I sleep. Thou art about my bed; defend me, O God, from all dangers which may happen to the body, and from all evil which may assault and hurt the soul. Spare me, if it be Thy good pleasure, to another day. May I awake up to praise Thee and to serve Thee better than I have ever before done.

Of Thy goodness and mercy, be pleased, O Lord, to hearken to these my prayers for the sake of Jesus Christ, my only mediator and Saviour. Amen.

Our Father, etc.

The grace of our Lord, etc.

DURING A VOYAGE, FOR YOURSELF AND THOSE WHO SAIL
WITH YOU.

Almighty God, Who alone commandest the winds and
the waves, and they obey Thy voice, mercifully hear my
prayers, and deliver me and all who are in this ship from
the dangers of the sea and from all sad accidents. We are
not able to save ourselves from the least misfortune to
which we are liable; to Thy favour and protection I commend myself and others, our souls and bodies, and all that
belongs to us.

Lord, pardon our sins, turn away the judgment which
we justly deserve, prosper us in our voyage, bring us to
our haven in peace, and grant that we may, at last, reach
the land of eternal rest, through Jesus Christ our Lord.
Amen.

ON SAFE ARRIVAL AFTER A JOURNEY OR VOYAGE.

Accept, O Blessed Lord, my humble and hearty thanks
for Thy merciful preservation of me during the voyage (or
journey) which is now at a prosperous end. Thy fatherly
hand has been over me, Thy loving protection has been
round about me by day and by night.

O Lord, make me ever mindful of this, and of all other
Thy favour and goodness to me, Thine unworthy servant.
Help me, who have now once again been kept and upheld
by Thee, to show forth my thankfulness by leading a holy
and Christian life, and serving Thee faithfully the remainder of my days; through Jesus Christ, my only Lord
and Saviour. Amen.

ON FIRST SETTLING IN A NEW COUNTRY,

Almighty God, who fixest the bounds of our habitation
and blessest the homes of Thy people, be mercifully pleased
to let Thy loving presence be with me in my new dwell-
ing-place. Thou art the God who changest not; here and
everywhere Thou art the same. Give me sure trust and

confidence in Thee. May I here enjoy Thy blessing which is life, and Thy lovingkindness which is better than life.

Give me courage and cheerfulness, patience and hope. In every time of loneliness, and discouragement, and anxiety, may my trust be in Thee. Keep me from murmuring and unbelief and forgetfulness of Thee. May I set Thee, the Lord, always before my face. Though far removed from the restraints that may have been about me in my former home, yet may I be on my guard against everything that would dishonour or displease Thee. May I preserve a sense of God and religion in all places and companies. May I never be ashamed of Thee or of Thy service.

Prosper me in all my lawful undertakings; grant me all things that pertain to life and godliness; give me health of body and of soul. Help me to be contented and thankful in all circumstances. Sanctify to me both the successes and failures, the labours and the recreations, which are here to be my lot. May I not live for myself alone, but endeavour to do all the good I can, both bodily and spiritual, to my neighbours. Above all things, grant that I may seek first the Kingdom of God.

O Lord, bless and keep me. O Lord, lift up the light of Thy countenance upon me, and give me peace now and for evermore, through Jesus Christ my Saviour and Redeemer. Amen.

Our Father, etc.

The grace of our Lord, etc.

THE CHURCH AND EMIGRATION.

—•◇•—

The late ARCHBISHOP OF CANTERBURY issued in December, 1881, the following circular letter on the subject of the Church and Emigration:—

"My Reverend Brethren and my Brethren of the Laity,—I am anxious to direct attention, from a Christian point of view, to the vast movement of people which has for some years been going on between Europe and the British Colonies, and especially between England and America.

"Official returns show that during the first nine months of the present year 313,716 emigrants left the ports of Great Britain, nearly 200,000 of whom were British subjects. The destination of more than 158,000 of these emigrants was North America.

"It has been proposed that a systematic endeavour should be made to establish more direct communication than at present commonly exists between the Church at home and the Church in our Colonies and in America, with a view to the Christian welfare of the vast population which is continually passing westward from our shores.

"The proposal is in accordance with the recommendations adopted by the Lambeth Conference of 1878. It has obtained the hearty consent of many of the bishops and clergy of the Anglican Communion in our Colonies and in the United States, and I am anxious to commend it to the notice of the parochial clergy of England.

"The scheme, which is still in its infancy, is at present under the management of a joint committee appointed by the Society for the Propagation of the Gospel and the Society for Promoting Christian Knowledge. Its objects, in outline, are as follows:—

"(a) To supply the parochial clergy of England with accurate information respecting the various fields for emigration, including special reference to the religious and educational advantages which they severally possess.

"(b) To publish, in a cheap form, a series of simple handbooks for the use of emigrants to our different Colonies and to the United States, containing, together with other intelligence, correct information as to the clergy, churches, Sunday and day schools, etc., in the various places in which emigrants are now settling.

"(c) To make such arrangements as may be found possible for the due care of emigrants from England on their arrival in our Colonies and in the United States. This would include the provision of commendatory letters from the parochial clergy in England to the clergy in whose neighbourhood the emigrants propose to settle.

"Full information respecting the scheme can be obtained on application to the Rev. J. Bridger, Emigrants' Chaplain, St. Nicholas' Church, Liverpool, to whom all communications on the subject should be addressed.

"It is, I think, impossible to exaggerate the importance of this subject, and I therefore commend it to the earnest and prayerful attention of my brethren the parochial clergy of England and the laity of our Church.

"Lambeth Palace, December 20, 1881.

"A. C. CANTUAR."

PRINTED BY WILLIAM CLOWES AND SONS, LIMITED, LONDON AND BECCLES.

www.ingramcontent.com/pod-product-compliance
Lightning Source LLC
Chambersburg PA
CBHW021522090426
42739CB00007B/736